# Praise for *A Surfer's Guide to Property Investing*

'If you are an aspiring or seasoned property investor, you must read this book from cover to cover. Paul replaces confusion with confidence in all facets of investing in property and how to set your own life goals. It's no surprise that Paul has earned the trust of his clients and built a sterling reputation in his industry.'

**Aaron Christie-David**, Managing Director, Atelier Wealth

'Paul practises what he preaches and shows that his pragmatic approach can be used by all investors of all levels. Whether you are a time-poor professional or lack the confidence and knowledge to invest, this book proves it can be done – simply saying "it's too hard" is not the right approach. Paul shares how the mind is your asset and getting your mindset right is the start to building a successful portfolio. Further leveraging from professionals and not just the bank resonates the strategic and realistic way to enhance results and to ensure overall success with your property portfolio and happiness.'

**Jeremy Iannuzzelli**, Partner, Keshab Chartered Accountants

'This book is an essential guide for any property investor. It covers all the fundamentals of property investing and the life skills you need to ride the wave of your life.'

**Ross Le Quesne**, Mortgage Broker, Aussie – Parramatta and Rouse Hill

'A beautiful, passionate and personal journey from Paul, with years of wisdom and practical guidance… from beginning to sophisticated investors, residential to commercial properties, working through the mindset to budget, to compliance, to legal, to growth and exit strategies, micro and macro determinants – the book is full of tips and real-life balanced current examples. I strongly recommend this as a tangible and motivational book for people in any stage of their lives!'

**Munzurul Khan**, Principal – Keshab Chartered Accountants

'This book is an inspirational story of what it truly takes to achieve success in property investment. Paul's professionalism and objectivity have extended into great insights in this terrific book.'

**Alex Veljancevski**, Principal Eventus Financial

T0359496

# A SURFER'S GUIDE TO PROPERTY INVESTING

# A SURFER'S GUIDE TO PROPERTY INVESTING

## THE NEXT WAVE

**How to achieve your financial goals and lead your best life through investing in property**

## PAUL GLOSSOP

MAJOR
STREET

Published in 2024 by Major Street Publishing
info@majorstreet.com.au | majorstreet.com.au

A catalogue record for this book is available from the National Library of Australia.

Printed book ISBN: 978-1-923186-21-7
Ebook ISBN: 978-1-923186-22-4

Cover design by Typography Studio
Internal design by Production Works
Printed in Australia by Griffin Press.

10 9 8 7 6 5 4 3 2 1

# Foreword

**Work hard... you'll eventually find your perfect wave.**

Surfers have a particular nostalgia when it comes to 'the search'. If you don't know what I'm referring to, this is the search for the perfect wave. 'The search' means a whole lot more, however. It's the process of getting there and the memories that keep you hungry for more.

As a Sydneysider, for me it's turning right onto the M1 from the Pacific Highway and heading north – the classic Aussie road trip – and the anticipation of good times, good laughs, good waves and cold beer. It's getting off the grid and leaving the responsibilities of an adult life behind – albeit just briefly.

Paul's story, like that of surfers the world over – and in particular those whose job often involves a suit from nine to five – evokes this spirit of exploration, the Holy Grail of family, work-life balance, happiness and fulfilment we all aspire to but rarely attain.

This is the real search. And his vehicle is property investment.

Creating wealth through property is no secret. Generations have capitalised on Aussie real estate, created wealth and built futures. It's the process of getting there that gives a reward at the end.

Myself, I have a detached view towards property: it's an asset I use to elevate myself to a future that will give me choice to do what I want to do. I don't get too emotional about property; it's its utility that resonates.

I'm not yet sure what this future is going to be, but I know property will certainly help me get there if I make informed decisions along the way, implement the correct strategies and use the right people. A big part of this is education – and I've read a few property books in my time. A number are excellent, some good; there are also a lot that are not so good.

Paul's book *A Surfer's Guide to Property Investing* resonated with me – not only as a very average surfer but as a process-driven person who appreciates the journey of making the right decisions at the right time to obtain an outcome – in this case, wealth creation through property investment.

For the 10 to 20 seconds you might get on a wave, a lot of hard work needs to be done. It's not unlike property. Swell direction, wave size, tides, weather and wind are all variables outside of your control. Your fitness, mental attitude, strategy (where to surf) and support network (making time) are all within your control to help you score that perfect wave.

With investing, bank policy, regulation, market fluctuations, politics, tax rules and reform are all the stuff you can't control. Your attitude, your strategy, your energy, your capacity to borrow, your advisers – these are all the things you can control.

Whether you surf or not, Paul's story as a property investor turned property professional is a great read. Draw on his story as you shape your own journey through property. Remember, you get out what you put in. If you're willing to do the hard work – and embrace the journey – you'll find your perfect wave.

*Phil Tarrant*
Managing Director, Momentum Media

# Contents

# Preface

I wrote the first edition of *A Surfer's Guide to Property Invest-ing* back in 2019. Little did I know at the time we were on the precipice of what would be the greatest global health crisis in living memory.

I wrote my book from a place of experience, knowledge and emotion about my philosophies for achieving financial freedom – but it was framed by a long period of relative normalcy.

Yes, we'd experienced market fluctuations in the preceding decades. There had been upheavals fuelled by events like the global financial crisis (GFC), and the mining boom and its subsequent bust. These were on my radar, of course, but no one could have reasonably predicted something like COVID-19. The pandemic resulted in worldwide social, political and financial disruption the likes of which we haven't seen since perhaps the Great Depression of the 1930s.

So, I shared my theories around wealth building oblivious to the fact that all my musings were about to be tested in the most spectacular fashion.

What I'm pleased to report is that my fundamental beliefs about building wealth through property investment held fast during those trying times. The foundations laid out in each chapter were solid, and my approach proved secure.

There was another element of the pandemic years from 2020 to 2024 that was also a kind of present – albeit one delivered in unusual wrapping. It was the gift of knowledge.

You see, society's immediate response to the pandemic challenge shaped our markets, but so too did the aftermath. Since 2020 we have witnessed shutdowns and stimuli, and razor-thin interest rates of 0.1 per cent which would go on to increase forty-fold in the ensuing months. Inflation spiked to record levels, 'cost of living' became a runaway train and employment numbers threatened to unravel.

Even now (mid 2024) there's uncertainty surrounding the global impact from nations at war, and there are world-changing elections on the horizon that will have a real and lasting effect on Australia's economic health.

The past four years have again demonstrated the resilience of property as an asset class, but they've also taught us all (including me) some important real-life lessons about investing.

It's for these reasons that I felt it crucial to update and expand upon my original book.

This latest edition of *A Surfer's Guide to Property Investing* weaves new information into the text to elevate its important teachings. There's also an entirely new chapter where I explore the upheaval we have experienced. I've had an opportunity to dissect the pandemic and its aftermath, study the various ways markets were affected, and investigate how the economy and investor sentiment responded.

My solemn wish is for readers to benefit from what we've learned during this disaster and its repercussions.

For me, it's all part of having a healthy mindset – don't look back on what's happened as just a global event of extraordinary proportion. Think of it also as an opportunity to grow wiser as an investor. As history has shown time and again, it's during periods of hardship that some of our greatest triumphs emerge.

*Paul Glossop*

# PART I
# FINDING THE PERFECT WAVE

# 1

# My story

I believe the key to financial success isn't about getting bigger, better, faster or more. To me, success is freedom – freedom to spend more time with my family or to give back to my community or, as you may have guessed from the title of this book, just to have more time to go surfing.

I've worked out through my life experiences that success is all about setting your barometer (see Chapter 3). This is an ethos I subscribe to wholeheartedly. It helps me make great decisions that pay both emotional and financial dividends now and in the future.

My barometer tells me that my family and I don't need expensive toys to have a fulfilling life.

We don't mark the success property investing has brought us by buying a fancy car or going on a $50,000 holiday to the Maldives. For us, success is marked by enjoying a simple life, with time for the things we hold dear – like family – and the freedom to decide where to direct our energy. We don't complicate our life with things that don't mean anything to us.

My wife Kim and I asked ourselves, 'Who do we really aspire to be?' And we decided the answer was that we aspire to be people who can give back to our kids, give back to community and just have time on our side. Once we determined that, it was time for me to take a calculated risk and walk away from a corporate career so I could start something that I was truly and holistically passionate about: helping my family and others change their lives through property.

Ultimately, that's what this book is about. Not every investor is looking to own a private jet. Many of the smartest individuals I know set their barometer at a realistic level of 'happiness' and forge on with the view that property provides freedom to enjoy the thing in life we all miss most – time.

Setting your barometer doesn't mean aiming low either, of course! My barometer helped me climb from zero assets to 17 property holdings worth almost $9 million in 10 years.

With the additional strategy of creating a development company and acquiring complementary assets both personally and within a self-managed superannuation fund over the past four years, my total portfolio value has now risen to approximately $50 million. This is hugely satisfying, as it not only ensures my wife and I have the means to live the life we want but also establishes a path for generational wealth to benefit our kids and grandkids.

This book is about where you are, where you want to be and how you're going to get there. And best of all, you and I are going to go on this journey together. I will show you how to build a property portfolio with the right mix of cash-flow, blue-chip and development opportunities – all designed to balance your wealth and your lifestyle.

I'll show you how to build a portfolio over time that doesn't involve lucking out in a fast growth market, but instead relies on a reasoned approach to sensible gains, all designed to set you free.

But first, here's a bit of background to my story.

## It's where you start

The right take-off point is vital. Every time I head out for a surf, I always spend some time scanning the line-up to find the best place to jump in and to position myself to catch the best waves on offer.

How you lead your life is defined to a great extent by your values. When you start to consider the values that define you, inevitably you think back to the people, places and events of your youth. That's where I'll start in sharing my life's journey with you – well, the journey this far anyway.

I was brought up in Liverpool, in southwest Sydney, by a single mum who made it a mission to ensure her boy entered the big wide world with all the emotional resilience, character and adventurous spirit he could muster without coming to grief along the way – untethered young men like to flirt with disaster, after all.

Our home life was a long way from the silver-spooned fortunes some broods enjoy in this harbour city – but it turns out that love, support, direction and motivation were better than a trust fund for me.

My mum raised me single-handedly and she was never the type to wallow. There was no point whingeing; she just got on with it. She's been my mentor in everything I've done – personally and in business. Mum studied as a nurse, then after a lifetime in the one profession, she retrained to become a post-natal-depression psychologist when she was in her fifties – talk about re-inventing yourself! She worked in this profession for over a decade before 'retiring' to a life filled with charity work and grandchildren. To me, she remains a testament to pursuing joys over riches.

Our family was sports mad, and I couldn't get enough of it. Mum was hell-bent on making sure I chased any activity with a passion. I spent the best part of my teenage years enjoying different athletic adventures. While schoolwork wasn't entirely left behind, it did come in second place behind my favourite physical pursuits. Like most of my friends, I had my sport, and would then get by with whatever grades kept me out of the principal's office.

Just before I turned 11, there was a defining tragedy in my life: my cousin, who was a really close friend, died of a stroke at age 15.

She had a predisposed heart condition, which hadn't been fully diagnosed. One school holiday, while we were visiting my auntie in Taree, all of us kids went to the lake in Forster. One moment we were enjoying ourselves as only kids can – all together, and swimming – and then just like that she was gone.

It was significant because things suddenly got real for me at an age when I should have been more concerned about the trivialities of life, like fixing a broken bike chain or scoring an extra slice of cake. I was fortunate to have a very, very tight-knit family, all dealing with this personal tragedy, and I just had to find my place among the grief.

A few months after that, my parents separated.

When it rains, it pours – but you can either stand still and get drenched or start hunting for cover.

## Choose to be resilient

My mum was now a single woman on a single wage with a big mortgage – but that didn't stop her. She had things to get on with. She got busy paying off the mortgage, raising her boy and realising life is what you make it.

Watching how she dealt with the hurdles and the confidence she displayed to stay on track is ultimately what drives me. It taught me that there are always going to be curveballs, just as there are always going to be opportunities, whether they are in relationships, investing, your career – whatever. In these situations you can take one of two possible paths. You can say, 'Look, life sucks, I'm done', or you can say, 'Life sucks, but I can make it better'. I learned to take that second path and just get on with it, reflect on what happened and move forward, because when it comes down to it, success is a decision to be resilient.

Mum also showed me that rewards are no fun if they're too easy. Whether you're talking tech in Silicon Valley, property cycles, manufacturing money in cryptocurrencies, or whatever it looks like, I think unless you've had the experience of earning rewards through hard yakka, you'll never fully appreciate your achievements.

It's something that my mum spent a lifetime teaching me.

## U-turn at the pub

Dramatic events have long-term consequences, and not all of them are bad. Life's turning points are rarely gradual – most are more than 90 degrees.

My career's sliding-door moment came one night at a pub in Ultimo, Sydney.

I was interested in architecture throughout my late teens, and I ended up heading to architectural college for two years after leaving school. My most important piece of assessment involved designing a five-storey office block with some spanking new software called AutoCAD, using top-notch laptop hardware. It was all borrowed from the university and the project took up pretty much the entire 12 months of my second year.

It was November 2002, and before submitting this mammoth assignment, my classmates and I decided to go for a couple of drinks at The Broadway Hotel to celebrate completing the work. We were sitting there, having a beer, talking about our assignments: what we did, how long it took us, et cetera, et cetera... and my laptop bag was at my feet under the table. I got up to get the next round, then settled down to polish off my schooner. Then it was time to go and submit my work. I looked down and my bag was gone. I thought my mates were pranking me, but that wasn't the case.

My bag containing the laptop and 12 months' worth of hard work got stolen in the few minutes that I wasn't watching it. This was before external hard drives and cloud storage. I had no back-up, so I was devastated.

I had a chat with my lecturer and the dean, and while they were sympathetic, they both said there was little they could do because without a submission there was no way to assess my progress. I needed to either figure out how to put my assignment back together, which would have been six months' more work, or start the whole course again. In the end, I decided a career in architecture was just not meant to be.

That was the catalyst for me to look at a career in teaching. Three-and-a-half years later I held a Bachelor of Education degree. I was a qualified teacher, but still wasn't convinced I wanted to be an educator. I was also keen to explore what the rest of the world had to offer.

## Heading overseas

With a few hundred dollars in my pocket, I jumped on a plane to the UK and took up my first teaching post in one of the roughest, toughest schools in London… and loved it!

I was in my mid-twenties, experiencing a lot of different culture, doing a lot of travelling and really enjoying life. I was also promoted to several higher roles during my time at the school – probably because they couldn't attract any real talent if I'm being honest.

I ended up being made Head of Department within a year of being a teacher, which, in hindsight, was never a role that someone in my position should have had to take on. Along with the experience and memories that I gained overseas, there was something else exceptional that I brought home from London: my wife, Kim. Kim is a highly dedicated professional who is passionate about teaching. However, I didn't share her calling, so with 2008 presenting some exciting opportunities in post-GFC Australia, I decided another change was on the cards.

## A fortunate flight

It seems a little good luck can appear in the strangest ways. I was at the airport to catch my flight home from the UK with literally £25 in my pocket. I knew I was coming back to my mum's house, and I knew I had a lot of work to do to get my life back in order. I had enjoyed my time in the UK and had the Facebook feed to prove it, but I also needed a way to kick off the next phase of my life.

I was standing in line at Heathrow Airport ready to pick up my Qantas boarding pass for a very cheap flight that would see me transiting through China. Suddenly, Qantas staff were walking along the queue and making an extraordinary offer to passengers willing to forgo this now overbooked flight – a night at the Hilton hotel, a business-class upgrade on the next day's flight and a $1,000 cheque.

I'd never wanted to miss a flight so badly. I ended up staying the night at the luxury hotel and flying business class, both of which I'd never done before. After arriving in Sydney, I went straight to the Qantas office and cashed the cheque.

That's how I ended up back home with $1,040 to kick-start my future.

## The lucky country

Unlike the pessimistic outlook in Europe, there were some economic and social pluses in Australia at the time that signalled opportunities. There was a mining boom, comparatively low unemployment, reasonably low property prices and historically high rental yields. And my senses were primed to take advantage of this environment – all I needed was a steady income and a plan.

I'd taken a job with a pharmaceutical company and was earning a good salary. I was also absorbed in developing a property investor mindset (more about this in Chapter 3) through self-educating in real estate investment and knuckling down to work out how to acquire our first Sydney property holding.

Once I'd landed that first piece of real estate, I was hooked. I'd found my passion in property.

I took that passion and started analysing property markets in the major capital cities. Were there any chances in Brisbane, Melbourne or Sydney? Should I buy and hold, acquire cash flow, consider subdivision or bank for development?

Within eight years of being back on Australian soil, I took the big step of quitting my job. Our property portfolio was providing a passive income sufficient to support our lifestyle while also creating enough equity to fuel our ambitions.

It was December 2014 and we had two children by this stage, so you can imagine how many friends and acquaintances told me I was bonkers for walking away from a decent income. But I knew what could be achieved from investing because the people I respected most had taken risks and been rewarded.

Kim and I had also done a lot of planning and preparation before I took the leap into self-employment. In fact, without Kim's support, I wouldn't have done it. I couldn't have done it. She's been unwavering.

And our team effort is paying off handsomely. Recent years have demonstrated to us how the right foundation can amplify the results. Since 2019, our business, Pure Property Investment, has doubled in size and taken on additional buyers' agents to accommodate a range of investors. We have more and more clients looking to start their journey from price points as low as $300,000. We're seeing increasing numbers of mid-range investors seeking long-term, high-quality, set-and-forget assets. We've also been growing our commercial property investment division, our property development arm and advisory around investing through self-managed superannuation funds. All of this during and post-pandemic.

COVID-19 has taught us that a focus on long-term goals stops you from getting sidetracked by market changes that are outside your control. Booms and busts come and go, but concentrating on a 15- to 20-year plan ensures you can weather almost any storm and reap the rewards.

## Chapter Hacks

- Set your barometer and align your goals with it.
- Understand your values.
- Learn resilience.
- Deal with hurdles head on – and keep on going.
- Make the most of lucky breaks, and follow your passion.
- Appreciate the guiding influences in your life.
- Keep your eye on the long-term horizon.

# Why property?

There are myriad investment vehicles out there hoping to attract your hard-earned dollars with the promise of future wealth, so why should property be top of your list?

In my experience, real estate is streets ahead (excuse the pun!) in three key areas:

1. predictable performance
2. leverage
3. control.

## Predictable performance

In my mid-teens, I distinctly remember one outcome of my parents' divorce was that mum paid out dad, as part of the settlement, so she could keep the family home.

My folks bought that house in Sydney's western suburbs in the early 1980s for $35,000. The market hadn't seemed to show a hell of a lot of growth, even after my mum became the sole owner. We even went through the staggeringly high interest rates of up to 17.5 per cent in 1987 and 1988, which caused many property owners no end of heartache, and some even to lose their homes.

Then, as if all of a sudden, it was 1993 and a revaluation of the home revealed its worth was $200,000. Nowadays that home would be worth closer to $850,000.

It struck me, even back then, that it took little effort to achieve that big result in capital growth. I thought, *Geez, that's a lot of money – that's crazy how much that property has gone up. You bought it for that and it's now worth this!*

This was the first time I took note of the consistent performance of property values.

I've since spent a fair bit of time studying shares versus property. The Australian Securities Exchange (ASX) index at the time of writing (July 2023) is 32 per cent higher than 10 years ago. Sounds great – but in comparison, Sydney's average home value over that same period has risen 104 per cent, and if you chose your real estate asset wisely, you would have far exceeded this performance. With the right strategy in place, real estate doesn't have to be a burden on your cash flow either.

If your risk profile is on the low side, riding the waves of share price peaks and troughs is more a horror than a thrill. For long-game investors, property has shown a steady and consistent value growth cycle without the dramatic ups and downs. That's hard to beat!

## Leverage

One of the secrets to building long-term wealth across any investment type is compounding interest. Combine that with the ability to leverage (borrow against) your holding and you can watch your personal balance sheet skyrocket.

When I first considered the value gain on my mum's house, I was too young to understand leveraging and compounding growth, so I decided to learn more about it. (If there are terms in this book that you aren't familiar with, just look in the glossary at the back.)

It didn't take long to grasp that if you've got equity in a property, it can be leveraged – and if you can afford the repayments, why not recycle that money?

For me, that was a lightbulb moment. While my career as an investor and adviser had not yet begun – in fact it was still some years away – the seed had been sown. I had realised there was a way to own property and build a portfolio without having to put down a hell of a lot of cash up front. You could extract equity from an asset and then recycle that equity into other holdings that could grow in parallel, thus creating a diverse, successful investment portfolio.

## Control

The final attraction that property provides, for an investor like me, is control.

Mum's home was our solid foundation. As long as she could manage the repayments on the home loan and the costs of necessary maintenance, she would not only provide a roof over our family's head, she'd also have a secure asset for her future.

You can invest in property, you can invest in shares (also known as equities) and you can invest in businesses. There are upsides to each of these choices but, in the end, with your properties you're the one in charge. You have a tangible asset, which is also always going be a saleable asset. Compare that to a business investment, where bad decisions – irrespective of whether they are made by a CEO or someone else – could cause that business to sink rather than surf. These bad decisions could potentially affect your stake in the business, and you would have little to no control over that.

## Investing fundamentals

One of the great things about the real estate investing community is it's a broad church. The investor enclave comprises a diverse cross-section of people – from first-time purchasers, to middle-aged mums and dads, to those contemplating their imminent retirement, and everyone else along this spectrum.

Investors have a variety of risk tolerances too. While some may be happy to snap up whatever is on offer, paddling fast and hoping they're perfectly positioned, others will be more clinical in their research and decision-making, allowing waves of opportunity to pass them by while they keep a keen eye on the conditions with a plan to jump on the ride of their lives.

Whether you're an early or late investor, have a high or low risk tolerance and are looking for blue-chip or more affordable locations, there are four fundamental philosophies that I think you should understand to elevate your chances of building a cracking property portfolio.

### 1. Timing is everything

There are two great regrets I commonly hear from seasoned property investors:

1. I started too late.
2. I sold too soon.

The former can be remedied by looking at my steps for learning how to adopt the winning investor mindset (see Chapter 3). The latter is often a result of not accepting that property is a long-term investment. Long-term investors are the folks who sit at the pointy end of the plane.

Most investors looking for solid gains across their portfolio's lifetime need to be in it for the long haul. Buying quality property with the right ingredients means sometimes you can ride a rising market wave and profit quickly – just ask Sydney property owners who bought in 2011. However, if you look back over the 15-year period in the run-up to 2011, you'll find growth in Sydney property values lagged other capital cities for most of a decade before it had its boom run. For those who held on even longer, the 2020 and 2021 bump elevated their gains exponentially.

Big money comes from patience; you need to allow compound growth to do its thing over the long term. (More about compound growth later.)

Be prepared to resist the temptation to make a 'fast buck' and sell too soon.

## 2. Nothing beats location

You can't out-train a bad diet, and you can't sweeten a property lemon.

It's fine to have the big home with the tasty finishes, but if it's positioned on a main road in an isolated suburb with an oversupply problem then your chances of realising a great return are limited.

Location is the key to success because it's of 'limited supply' and can't be changed regardless of how much money, time and effort you have at your disposal.

Make sure you research your locations well, looking at region, suburb, street and individual property to ensure you maximise your chances. (There's more about picking the right location in Chapter 7.)

## 3. The nation is your market

Real estate in Australia has evolved at a rapid pace over the past 20 years.

Ask your elders (for millennials, this means anyone over the age of 45) about where they were most likely to invest two decades ago. The vast majority – if not all – would say the suburb they lived in or, if not their home suburb, certainly somewhere within their home city.

Today, it has never been easier to be a borderless investor, capable of seeking out markets anywhere across our broad, brown land. There is a wealth of information readily available online and a growing number of professionals capable of helping you study and acquire an investment property in a multitude of areas.

Don't limit your thinking to tracking those five suburbs you know and love, where you used to ride your bike and play street cricket. Broaden your horizons and take advantage of all the real estate that's on offer.

## 4. Free your mind – the rest will follow

I understand the concepts of gut instinct and emotional connection. They can be important tools when you need to react quickly to the question, 'Should I stay or should I go?' To be a successful investor, however, the numbers must make sense first.

As a fundamental, I implore you to run through the figures carefully before making decisions that will affect your financial security. Start with your home budget and make sure you won't go broke – or at least, have a buffer – if you must take on a higher level of risk. Check your loan commitments and ability to deal with a mortgage.

Check and recheck the figures on properties you are interested in investing in, too. Don't just take an agent's word for it. Do your own research into rental income and comparable property values. Do they all make sense?

Get the numbers right so you can rely on your heart and gut without fear when opportunity presents itself.

## Chapter Hacks

- Remember the big three property positives: predictable performance, leverage and control.
- Absorb the fundamentals of investing in property, including timing, location, mindset and the numbers.

# PART II
# BEFORE YOU PADDLE OUT

# Mastering the investor mindset

The thing that sets successful property investors apart from property dabblers is mindset.

It's the surfing equivalent of paddling onto a seven-foot monster wave for the very first time. The battle between your ears can have you either sliding gracefully down the face and ready for a bottom turn or tumbling awkwardly over the falls contemplating a few minutes without oxygen.

The right mindset allows you to approach investing in a methodical, strategic fashion so you can make rational decisions that will yield long-term benefits.

Australians have long had an affinity with the dream of owning a home in the suburbs, so it can be difficult for some investors to break free from that romantic notion and look at real estate based on cold, hard facts – but realism is essential if you want to get ahead.

A good example is the real estate development I completed a couple of years ago.

One of the new homes we built in this project is our current family home. We're a beach-loving crew, so we'd been renting close to the water before this home was built. I know that financially it makes far more sense to rent a property by the beach than own by the beach. That's the way it's always been for me – the numbers have to stack up.

Our new home meets the emotional needs of the family. Kim and the kids see being close to school and friends in a beautiful home as a driving factor, but for me it had to make sense as an investment as well as a home. I knew at the time this development would have a 30 per cent return on investment, so I was happy to proceed. We ended up with all those emotional factors covered, plus a beautiful family home within walking distance of the beach, while at the same time making money.

As you can see, even when planning a new abode, I carry my investor mindset with me.

I think the mentality of home ownership will be turned on its head over the next few generations. My children will be growing up in a society where large, detached housing in prime suburbs will essentially be unattainable, but they'll adapt. The next generation may consider it entirely valid to live in a unit their whole lives, or even rent forever. These scenarios will become the new normal.

The first signs of adaptation are already evident, with the more entrepreneurially minded millennials 'rentvesting'. This wasn't even a word before 2012. The idea that you should rent where you want to live for lifestyle reasons and invest in growth zones is confounding to most non-investors aged over 50.

Rentvesting is now one of many ever-more imaginative paths to investing in property as society evolves and adapts. Think fractional ownership or even co-buying with friends – these are evolving options for first-time owners.

The common theme for me is that even if you are taking off on a six-foot gem, there will be a point when you want to either speed up or carve off the lip, and the best way forward is never in a straight line. To find success in the future, savvy thinkers will need to adopt the investor mindset and find imaginative ways to achieve their goals.

## Recognising the mindset

In my professional life, I've met a range of people from diverse educational and social backgrounds. They can't all be lumped under one generic description, defined by the hand they've been dealt. It's ridiculous to say the London teenager I met in my teaching job is destined to fail because of his hard-knocks upbringing, or that the highly educated PhD graduate has answers to life's toughest questions given his extraordinary intellect.

Those who reach a measure of success come from all walks of life, but I have found two common traits among the people I know with the investor mindset: they all demonstrate control and responsibility.

## Control

I was discussing the attraction of nine-to-five occupations with a fellow professional. We came to the conclusion that workplaces create a false sense of security. They are designed to promote a supposedly anxiety-free lifestyle, but that's an illusion, which in some respects is stifling employees' full potential across a multitude of aspects in their daily lives.

I've worked for big corporations. In these businesses, many employees know the 'when' – when to turn up, when to do their job, when to go home and when the pay will arrive in their bank account. They operate feeling secure in their roles, but it doesn't take much of a shift in economic fortunes for them to realise the rug can be pulled from under their feet at any time – even in a seemingly secure professional environment.

The perfect example of this is when the pandemic hit in early 2020. In the space of just a few weeks, hundreds of thousands of people lost work. Companies with full order books went into shutdown and the queues started to mount at Centrelink. One thing I did notice from this time is that those who had control over their professional lives were more likely to survive. The people I mix with in small business were able to take steps to ensure they could carry on once the dust settled – things like choosing to reduce their own take-home pay from their business or working exclusively from their home desk. They could put themselves in caretaker mode for as long as necessary. Those without control (employees) found that a fast edict from the executive could leave them without a job at a moment's notice, and many were left wondering how they'd survive.

In my opinion, successful people seize control. They take responsibility and own their successes and failures. Planning is key for them, and they leave little to fate.

## Responsibility

People who achieve success never blame the environment. They never blame someone else. Ultimately, they make the decisions. They're in charge.

Even if they're employing someone to do something on their behalf, successful people take responsibility. They don't let anything get in the way. They say, 'I am responsible, and I know that I am responsible, and I'm not going to blame anyone if something goes south. Nor will I thank anyone if something goes north. Because you know what? I did it.'

Not only will this sort of thinking free you from the fallacy that an employer or the government owes you financial support, but it will also open a door to the possibilities of success and generate respect among your peers.

Ultimately, you are the master of your destiny, and until you understand that you are in control, you will not effect change, neither for yourself nor in people around you. If it is to be, it is up to me.

## Seven steps to achieving the investor mindset

I believe gaining the investor mindset and preparing your mettle for becoming the master of your destiny is a conscious decision. Here are seven steps to help you get there.

### 1. Set your barometer

Not everyone wants a bigger boat – in fact, most people don't even need one.

Step one towards achieving an investor mindset is to set your barometer. It is the key take-off point for your investment journey, and your future self will thank you for making time to define this first. To set your barometer, you need to ask yourself:

- Who are the people who make me happy?
- Do I spend enough time with them?
- What have been the moments that have brought me the greatest joy?
- How will life change over the next one, three, five, seven and ten years?
- Can I imagine looking back with regret at opportunities missed and moments lost?
- Are there decisions I can make now that 'future me' will be thankful for?

Take time to decide what type of people you and your significant other are, and think hard about what you need now and in the future to help you build upon those traits to make you a complete person (achieving success through following your passions, in the company of loved ones).

I know from my own experience that Kim and I want a life that affords us time. We don't want to be tethered to a nine-to-five existence. We want to be the captains of our own ship. This will give us the chance to watch our kids grow into whatever lies ahead – safe, secure, cared for and well educated in all life has to offer. I know this will eventually see them grow into independent and capable human beings.

This is our barometer. By setting our barometer and aiming for our higher goals, we've gained the ability to fulfil our dreams. And while it's possible to still enjoy the 'toys' if we choose, they aren't the ultimate recognition of our achievements.

By the way, our journey is far from over. But we've realised that the key is being true to ourselves and what we're passionate about in life.

Set your barometer first so you don't look back in anger and regret.

## 2. Set your goals

Once you've discovered what makes you – or will make you – the best you can be, start considering which goals to aim for. Ask yourself these questions:

- At what age would I like to stop work?
- Do I want to stop work at all?
- How much income do I realistically need to live a fulfilled life?

Some people love what they do and never want to stop working. I just believe you should work because you want to, not because you have to. In terms of an income goal, many might believe the magic figure is $100,000 per year, but if you own your home outright and aspire to nothing more than freedom to jump in the car and travel north/south/east/west, then you may need far less.

Now is also a time to think about what lies ahead. For instance:

- Are my kids graduating into high school soon?
- Am I about to become an empty nester?
- Do I want to spend my time and energy building something brilliant?
- Do I want to try new experiences that will realistically require years to plan?
- Do I want to run the Boston Marathon? (Cool, but you've got to make plans around that.)
- Would I like to create my own not-for-profit organisation that builds schools in Cambodia? (Magnificent, but you need to get your actions in focus.)

Write down all those things that will be benchmark moments in your life in the next five to ten years and beyond. These are the goals that require effort and forward thinking.

## 3. Create a scratch map

A scratch map is a timeline of when those things you've been planning are going to happen. Mark down when you're retiring and when the kids move out. Make a note of when those big events will occur.

Building a timeline helps bring most strategies into sharp focus. You may have plenty of time on your side… or you might discover you don't have as much time as you thought.

By looking carefully at where you want to be, and the joys, opportunities and hurdles that lie ahead, you'll start to focus on the right investment strategies to help you achieve your best life.

## 4. Educate yourself

There has never been a better time to get educated on the world of property and finance.

The amount of information available online and throughout the media is incredible. Almost anyone who has an opinion on property has a forum to discuss, argue and agree on ideas. Browse the various groups and see what discussions are trending. Check if there are local meet-ups for real-estate-interested folk in your area. You never know who you might meet who will change your life.

Also, get out there and hit the ground running. Attend open homes, enjoy auctions and talk with agents, valuers and just about anyone else you can find who has a property brain.

Don't just concentrate on learning the success stories. I think anyone who tells you they have a magic real estate investment strategy that provides a risk-free way for you to live your dreams is probably trying to sell you something. Others have made mistakes in the past – learn from them instead of making them again yourself. Property nightmares exist, and knowing about even one can save you hundreds of thousands of dollars in bad investing.

Learning from mistakes is imperative to developing the investor mindset, because your journey will have ups and downs, triumphs and challenges. Properly internalising this mindset includes being able to deal with the risks as well as the rewards. There are many property investors out there who wish they hadn't sold in a flurry of fear. Long-term strategies require a landlord's faith in the adage that extended time in the market will become your best-ever investment.

## 5. Mentor up

Finding a mentor helps create some certainty in an environment where you must expect the unexpected.

Mentors come in all forms. Family members and friends who have already completed their investing journey can help you wade through the vagaries of what lies ahead. The best thing is that most mentors from this pool are trustworthy and have your best interests at heart. The downside is that some family will not be on board when it comes to property investment. These people will oversell the horror stories of investments gone bad and help you relive the lousy times they've had in real estate. Constructive caution is fine; destructive horror tales that halt you in your tracks are not.

Of course, you can look outside your family for mentors. Some investors are willing and able to help answer tough questions and give you realistic perspectives and expectations about property investing. These may be in the fold you encounter online or at regular property investment group meet-ups. Many will be experienced and happy to share wisdom out of the goodness of their hearts, but be careful: these forums and groups can also include unscrupulous operators looking to sell their own wares or wrap you up in schemes that you'd be better to avoid, so tread warily.

Finally, there are the professional property mentors who will represent you and advise you for a fee. Buyer's agents, valuers, investment advisers and the like can assist you in the planning and process of building a portfolio. The key is to ensure their strategy aligns with your own. These professionals should work hard to help you achieve your objectives by walking you through the process. They can not only help you gain the investor mindset but also ensure you buy the right types of property for your portfolio.

My caveat in seeking a mentor is to be cautious – this water is full of sharks. Check the conditions and proceed with safety. Do some research on any mentors or advisers you have shortlisted. Try to find an independent referee who's already surfed these waves.

Here's something better – contact professional bodies such as the Property Investment Professionals of Australia (PIPA) or the Real Estate Buyers Association of Australia (REBAA). Members of these organisations are required to comply with a code of conduct to help protect consumers.

## 6. Surround yourself with success

I believe in the old adage that you are a product of your five closest friends. These are the family you choose and they have a profound effect on how your life will track.

I choose friends and acquaintances who reflect virtues and attributes I aspire to have myself. It certainly is a case of keeping up with the Joneses, but in this instance, you get to select the Joneses who set your benchmarks.

Having a close-knit community that elevates you and helps inspire you to be your best 'you' will solidify your investor mindset. It will boost your chances of being not only a successful real estate investor but also a well-rounded human being.

## 7. Recognise what you don't know

Self-aware investors have the mature reasoning to realise they don't know everything.

In 1974, a psychologist named Paul Slovic did a study that demonstrated something called confirmation bias. It's a really important concept to understand in the context of property investing.

Slovic wanted to study the effect of information on decision-making, so he selected a group of eight horse handicappers – those who help determine odds of horses winning races – and set them a task. He asked the group to pick the winners of 40 races. For each race he varied the amount of information he provided on the runners.

In the first race, each handicapper could choose five pieces of information on each horse from the range of available data (how experienced the jockey was, the fastest run recorded for a horse, and so on). Slovic also asked each handicapper to rate how confident they were in their prediction. In round one, armed with five pieces of information, 17 per cent of the group predicted the outcome and they were overall 19 per cent confident of their prediction. Pretty close.

However, as the study progressed, Slovic upped the amount of available information each handicapper could draw upon. The result? As they were fed more and more information about the horses, the handicappers became increasingly confident about their ability to pick the winner. In fact, their confidence doubled.

The interesting thing was their success at picking winners actually flatlined at around that 17 per cent mark. So, despite feeling better informed and more likely to make a correct choice, they actually weren't any better at picking winners.

Beyond a certain point, extra facts that don't agree with our original conclusions are conveniently 'ignored' while other information that does agree with our already adopted position is used to re-enforce our 'correct assessment'. This is called confirmation bias.

How does this apply to property investing? Well, confirmation bias suggests investors will try to unearth information that confirms their pre-existing beliefs and discount information that refutes them. This means unaware investors will ignore facts that could be useful in making the right decisions. The result: confirmation biases can lead to investors not making the best possible choices.

My advice for gaining the investor mindset is to have an open mind, and seek out people who think differently from you and other sources of information that are different from your own already established ideas. This will make you a wiser and better-informed investor.

## Remember to breathe

Before I leave the subject of mindset, I want to remind you that panic does you no good. It can suck the oxygen right out of your system; as any wave of uncertainty comes down on your skull, you can be left gasping for relief.

This feeling of panic is common for first-time investors in particular. Just remember – you're not the first to experience this. Relax, breathe and let the experts help guide you.

In my business, I see people panic all the time. I've even been guilty in the past of fuelling the panic that clients experience when they are making their initial forays into the world of property investing. As a devout property 'tragic', I have been known to get caught up in the process and vernacular of real estate, using terms and acronyms that can seem like a foreign language. This leaves clients who don't know their way around a dataset feeling unduly panicked. It can be confronting for the novice investor – and I've really tried to stop doing this!

Another way to avoid becoming panicked is to steer clear of the well-meaning, well-voiced but ill-informed opinions of those around you. These are family, friends and casual acquaintances who sow seeds of doubt about your decision to become a property investor. We've all heard them: 'Why are you doing this?' or, 'Why didn't you buy in this location instead of that location?' or, 'You should have bought shares' or, my least favourite, 'If only you'd bought and sold Bitcoin at the right time. You'd be loaded by now!'

Over time, I've learned the following techniques that property investors can rely on to keep them on track and make sure their thinking stays clear.

## Break it down

In the initial planning stages, when you're setting your investment goals, take some time to break down the steps – don't get too wrapped up in the one big number at the finish line.

Sure, in the end, you may be looking to create personal net wealth of $10 million, which sounds exciting and impressive... but can also appear daunting. My advice is not to focus on this overwhelming figure, but rather think about how you are going to get there. That final payday is the result of a plan that will take anywhere between 15 and 30 years to carry through. It's a long-term flag on the horizon – entirely achievable but not easily attained in a short timeframe.

Breaking that monster result into medium-term, achievable goals, which plot a practical path to what you want, relieves an awful lot of stress. Those mid-term goals answer questions like, 'How much?' or, 'How many?' or, 'What's the total portfolio going to look like?' in terms of three years from now, then five years, then ten years, and so on.

You can even break those planned mid-term achievements into specific short-term, practical steps. Ask yourself, 'What does my first step look like?' Based on your personal finances (which we'll discuss in Chapter 4) it might be investing in an affordable, high-yield, semi-regional location, or it could be buying a higher-priced growth asset. The decision will depend on your current situation and the path you've plotted to achieve your dreams.

You want to make sure this is where your focus is right now. If you follow the steps, the future will take care of itself.

## Flexibility is key

Remember that while having a comprehensive understanding of your strategy early on is important, not everything you decide on day one will remain as your plan evolves.

Truth be told, you're not going to decide exactly what properties, or how many or what value the holdings will be, as part of those mid-term goals. You'll have a reasonable idea about those things, but investing requires you to pivot quickly in response to changes in the market or economy, or to take up opportunities that present themselves. Deciding on exactly what and where to buy relies on an awful lot of crystal ball–gazing. Sticking rigidly to specifics decided on day one of your investment journey, and choosing to ignore the influences that progressively push and shove on your choices, is a recipe for disaster.

Don't fight the swell, just ride the wave.

## Zoom approach to sanity

Dealing with unexpected forces, whether positive or negative, requires what I call a zoom-in, zoom-out, zoom-in approach.

Let's discuss a simple example. You are happily watching your portfolio grow, but an extended period of vacancy hits one of your property holdings. You just can't seem to find a tenant because a major nearby employment source recently shut its doors. It's a shame because the analysis shows that as a long-term investment, this property is set to boost your wealth, because there are plans for major infrastructure in this area.

Your first reaction might be, 'Oh my God! Sell the thing! I can't afford to pay the loan with no tenants!' This is where you have 'zoomed in' on the problem property, causing your heart rate to race while fine beads of sweat break out on your furrowed brow. It's a natural reaction.

The solution is to 'zoom out'. Revisit your goals and strategy. Take a look at where you are in your journey. Re-study the steps that led you to where you are now. Think about how this property fits into your long-term goals. Is the plan to hold it for 15 years? Are the same economic fundamentals still in place, indicating this is an asset worth keeping in your portfolio? If so, then the answer isn't to offload but to look for a strategic solution.

This is where we zoom back in. Think about the property and the achievable rent. Will your financial buffers carry you through if you take on a new tenant at a reduced rent? Is there equity in the portfolio that can be drawn on to help prop up the holding over the short term so you can still enjoy the long-term payoff?

I've found that most hurdles can be cleared once you get into the habit of recognising an issue (zoom in), revisiting your goals (zoom out) and analysing your options (zoom in).

This approach works twofold as it also helps to deal with anxiety.

## A final word on why mindset is crucial

Given all this advice, you might feel that real estate investing is not in your sweet spot. I've seen it plenty of times before – in fact, I came across just such a case recently.

One of my client couples hasn't yet gained the mindset of long-term investors, of tolerating some risk now in order to achieve the life they want. I blame myself to an extent for their lack of enthusiasm for the subject, because part of my role is to educate them on the ways they can live the life they want through property. Perhaps I need a better whiteboard?

My clients bought a second-hand home as their first investment, and it has had some teething issues. It was only about eight months old and needed some running repairs, like waterproofing and lock replacement, that have set them back a few thousand dollars.

They were already hesitant about getting into real estate in the first place. I'd spent several hours with them going through scenarios and running plans to give them confidence. We'd discussed the importance of thinking long term – in fact, I'd advised them that this was a 20-year-plan they were taking on.

I'd also discussed the asset they were looking at. We had noted that it was an existing property that was neutrally geared (see the glossary) from the outset. We knew it would have some maintenance issues, and we factored those into their projected cash flow, allowing for a buffer to cover expenses. With cash flow, all investors have good years and bad years – it's swings and roundabouts.

Despite this, my clients had trouble seeing the big picture and now feel they've made a terrible mistake in deciding to buy a property which will cost them money to hold in a condition that allows it to generate a reasonable rental income.

It's a classic case of negative confirmation bias – and I take responsibility for that, because while I think they've bought the right asset for their plan, they weren't mentally in the right place to invest. Regardless of how much data or information I provided, they had already prepared themselves to reinforce their negative bias.

They effectively made the decision that the property would be a disaster, regardless of the outcome. They were waiting for something bad to happen so they could say, 'We knew we shouldn't have done this'. If you don't take time to establish the investor mindset and use mental tools to ensure you follow your plan, then you aren't going to be ready for property investing.

My one caveat is this piece of good news – most investors can acquire the right frame of mind to be successful investors. I would estimate around one in 50 people aren't able to become fully prepared, so those are pretty good odds.

It just takes effort, patience and some support from those around you.

## Chapter Hacks

- Successful people display control and responsibility.
- The seven steps to acquiring an investor mindset are to:
  1. set your barometer
  2. set your goals
  3. create a scratch map
  4. educate yourself
  5. mentor up
  6. surround yourself with success
  7. recognise what you don't know.
- Remember to breathe.
- Use the zoom-in, zoom-out approach to recognise an issue, revisit your goals and analyse your options.

# 4

# Budgeting and strategy

Those who want to surf should ideally first know how to swim. In a similar fashion, those who aim to be successful property investors should have a good understanding of their own personal budget before they start to formulate investment plans.

Smart investors choose to work closely with skilled mortgage brokers and financial advisers. But regardless of who you choose for your dream team (see Chapter 6), success requires the investor to reinforce their mindset around financial goals, strengths and limitations.

## Personal budget

Your personal or home budget should take pride of place among your fiscal considerations. A property investor's home budget should be a frank and fearless dissection of what it takes to run a household and not go broke.

There are plenty of budgeting tools available online to use to work out your world of dollars and where they're spent. Your talented mortgage broker will also help guide you through the personal budget process as part of your loan application.

A personal budget initially helps you track and report how each dollar of your income moves through your household. The great thing about budgets is that for many of us they become ingrained and automatic over time. I find, for example, that I no longer need to track my budget with surgical precision. How and where I spend my money to fulfil my family's wishes is now second nature. I've become holistically better at money management through achieving a necessary income, keeping an eye on my goals, regularly rechecking my personal barometer and making informed choices about where my dollars are used.

I think budgets help households prioritise money, and the flow-on is you gain an almost automatic ability to assess your spending habits each time you reach for your wallet.

While initially you might find yourself saying, 'According to my Excel spreadsheet I can only afford take away dinner twice this month. What a drag!', what eventually happens is you auto-matically prioritise the importance of what you're doing. You'll choose to have a takeaway dinner only once this month because your personal barometer already decided taking the family to see a live performance of the *The 143-Storey Treehouse* was a better use of your cash.

The nice thing is, when you get to grips with budgeting, you stop denying you and yours the important things in life and begin enjoying how you use your money, all the while watching your personal wealth increase through investing.

It's a pretty nice way to live.

## Journey planner

I always advise investors of the importance of developing the right mindset and setting goals to determine where the finishing line is. But typically, what is the process for defining a path once you understand where you want to end up?

Like any journey, knowing your destination is only part of the process, because the next step is formulating a plan to get there. Let's say – for argument's sake – to achieve your dreams you have to create $100,000 a year in passive income. What do you need to think about in order to forge your path? Start by taking stock of where you are now:

- What am I earning now?
- What is my total savings position?
- What are my present commitments (e.g. rent and/or mortgage repayments)?
- What expenses do I need to live, work and play?
- What's my superannuation position?
- How many years do I have until retirement?

By looking at your take-off point and compounding potential returns over the years you have until retirement, you have a better chance of determining where the likely shortfall is and how best to fill that gap.

If you've got your own home, how long is it going to take you to pay that off on your current income/s at your existing mortgage level? By calculating how long this will take, and allowing for your total savings and equity position, you can start to understand what sort of wealth you will need to build over the next few years to help you achieve your goal.

If you buy a $500,000 property now, based on say a 6 per cent annual capital growth rate, it would be worth $1,006,098 in 13 years. At a net (after costs) yield of 2.5 per cent, that reflects an annual income of $25,152 to you.

Consider how close this will get you to acquiring that $100,000 a year passive income. Based on these numbers, that investment is going to get you a quarter of the way there. So, theoretically, you need four of those assets in your portfolio – and to be mortgage-free too, of course.

You need to factor in all the variables. Figure out where you are now financially, how much you have in superannuation and how much it is going to take to pay off your home or continue to pay rent (if that's what you choose to do).

And then, from a property perspective, how many investments are you going to need to buy, what will their value be and what sort of rental return can you expect?

If you have a joint mortgage, you're going to have to discuss with the other mortgagor/s how you'll eventually pay down the mortgage or mortgages. Would you sell down the assets at a defined time and pay down the debt?

Finally, there are important decisions to make around ownership structures, pay-down methods, sell-down methods, the ramifications for capital gains tax (CGT), and all the other aspects that come with property investing.

As you can see, setting out an investing strategy is both complex and highly individualised, but the three essential elements remain the same:

1. Where do I start?
2. Where do I want to finish?
3. How will I get there?

It needs to be a really calculated, step-by-step process and requires you to be frank and open, laying all your cards on the table. Keep reading – this book can help you with each step along the way!

## Chapter Hacks

- Get to grips with your personal (home) budget before you start your investment journey.
- In order to formulate your investing strategy, you need to be crystal clear on your take-off point and destination.

# 5

# Learning and groundwork

Indulge me for a moment in a surfing metaphor.

Imagine you're just about to paddle onto your first six-foot peak. You've spent months gaining and honing the practical skills required to catch this wave. You've whiled away hours on the beach staring at breaks so you can read the run of the swell. You've prepared in small surf, tackling tiny but pushy crests to ensure your muscle memory is in order.

On the big day, you once again view the waterscape from the sand to pick the best paddle-out point. Then, when you're among the break, you take 15 minutes to position yourself to take advantage of the incoming set.

Once you've picked your wave, you paddle like hell to build up momentum and draw on all that hard yakka learned in the months leading to this moment so you can confidently conquer the swell.

This is it! The greatest day of your surfing life! You're up...

... and off!!! Fallen off...

Here's where the learning really begins, not ends, because as any enthusiastic, even mildly talented surfer will tell you, every wave holds a lesson. Perhaps you were too deep in the section?

Perhaps you misread the bank and the wall of water just disappeared? Perhaps you just didn't commit fully?

I reckon every time surfing legend Mick Fanning feels he 'failed' on a wave (as rare as that might be), he takes a few moments to analyse the outcome, form a solution and hope for an opportunity to apply this new knowledge.

Here's another thing you should note: from first-time grommets through to world champions, everyone who has ever succeeded in their goals – whether big or small – has adopted the mantra to never stop learning.

## Never stop learning

As we've already touched on, becoming a successful property investor involves not only absorbing information from various sources but drawing on the wisdom and support of others. Before we get into building your dream team of people who will help you achieve your property goals, I'd like to talk a bit about building up your real estate knowledge.

Some believe you can cut back on your education when you internalise the investor mindset and move closer to purchase. Many also subscribe to the idea that as you secure your initial property holding and look across your strategy, you can ease off on your self-schooling altogether and let the wave of investing do its thing.

This couldn't be further from the truth. Self-education should be an ongoing process, particularly in the dynamic sphere of real estate investing. You will gain a lot of knowledge about property and investing while you're building the investor mindset, but there is always plenty more to learn.

Be aware that confirmation bias can pull up a chair and mess with your 'bullshit filter' when you are gaining education. It's very easy to unearth opinions that reinforce your already long-held beliefs about property investing. This is a pointless exercise that, at its worst, can open you up to bad advice with catastrophic financial downsides.

Also remember that when it comes to receiving advice from your mentors and property investment advisers, one of the trickiest things to do is to be able to filter the good from the bad.

Keep reading, keep searching and keep devouring information, but apply a filter that enables you to run reality checks with a healthy dose of scepticism. Unfiltered information overload puts you at risk of progressively becoming mentally clouded. You may feel as if you started with a clear objective, but then – as an increasing number of conflicting opinions are thrown your way – find yourself more confused than you were in the beginning. This is particularly the case when you are dealing with property investment advisers who are looking to take you on as a client.

Here's my tip – look at how successful any adviser has become by applying their strategy to investing. It's not just their actions but also their results that speak louder than words.

When applying a filter to the advice you receive from mentors and other advisers, figure out who you want to be associated with and make sure you truly understand their motivations. Don't look for people who are going to kowtow to your opinion just because they want you as a client. They need to challenge you, and you want to be able to challenge them in return.

Be brave – diamonds are made under pressure.

## Four rules to building your dream team

Even if you're one of the fortunate few who seems innately talented at everything you attempt, there are many aspects of property investing that require a professional eye. It takes years, sometimes decades, of professional practice to acquire the skills necessary to be the very best. Fortunately, we live in the era of outsourcing, when you can hire your own experts to take care of the heavy lifting.

Dream team experts work hard to bring about the best possible outcome for you when you are on your investing journey. They are beholden only to you – their client.

Selecting the best team early in your investment journey is paramount. It takes work to build the right team of mentors and paid advisers (in Chapter 6 I'll give a rundown of the different team member roles), but if you make the effort to surround yourself with the best possible posse now, it will pay off handsomely in the long run.

Now you're ready to build your dream team, there are four rules I believe you should follow.

## 1. Look for experience

When it comes to the professionals in your dream team, such as your mortgage broker and your conveyancer, you want to be able to draw on and benefit from their experience. So, look for professional advisers who can demonstrate that they've not only faced the same hurdles you're likely to encounter, but they have also found solutions.

You should be looking for an accountant who understands property inside and out, and a well-informed local town planner. Your buyer's agents should understand the markets they're buying in, and your financial planner must understand insurances and protections specific to property.

One of the best five-word questions to ask any professional you're considering hiring is, 'Are you a property investor?' There's nothing like dealing with someone who has put their money where their mouth is.

It's even better when they've found a path that's led them or their clients past challenges towards success. Follow the 'wealth scout' approach and choose an adviser who has paddled out into a 10-foot storm swell so you can find the best take-off position.

## 2. Seek out communicators

It makes sense that you want the best possible people taking care of your business. Unfortunately, talent and communication skills don't always go hand in hand. I believe it is essential that your selected specialists can communicate with you and other members of your dream team simply and effectively.

The nature of the business is that you'll find yourself juggling a lot of balls and managing a gaggle of advisers whenever you look to secure a new property holding or manage your portfolio. It's in your best interests to be certain those specialists will be able to tell you what you need to hear, not what you want to hear.

One of the biggest frustrations that can befall an investor is to have a potentially profitable deal hit a wall because someone didn't make a phone call early enough.

I have fortunately had plenty of deals go through, both for myself and my clients, because the mortgage broker we use is so good at communicating. He's the sort of bloke who will get on the phone to the financier when it's time to check on key performance indicators (KPIs) in the process of securing a property. A few simple questions for the bank at the right time, such as, 'Has the valuation been completed yet?' or, 'When will the approval come through?' or even, 'What else do you need from me to make this happen?' can make the difference between success and failure.

This broker is also on hand to respond to and assist our conveyancing solicitor, accountant or any other member of the team who needs him.

Just ask anyone who's had a deal fall over because a bank 'jockey' forgot to order a valuation in time and no one chased them up, and you'll understand why good communicators are worth their weight in gold.

## 3. Avoid sharks

Here's another of the best short questions, five of the most powerful words an investor can put to a potential adviser: 'How do you get paid?'

There is often the risk of a conflict of interest for buyer's agents, selling agents, property investment advisers and even mortgage brokers, because whoever pays the adviser's fee usually has a stake in their advice. That's fine if they're beholden only to you for their fee, but if others are also filling their bank accounts, you need to wonder who they're looking after first and foremost.

Have you heard this version of The Golden Rule? 'Whoever has the gold, make the rules.'

When you are considering a prospective property investment adviser, for example, think logically about where they're suggesting you buy and what sort of product they're directing you towards. If they appear overly keen on you buying in a specific development in a particular location, then ask outright, 'How do you get paid?' I'd even suggest asking, 'Do you or your company receive any form of income from the developer/builder of this property?'

I was discussing this scenario with an associate who is a property valuer in Queensland. He'd been working in the far western suburbs of Brisbane during the 1990s, where a spate of duplex villas was being built and sold to Sydney investors. He and his associates had been taken aback by how much these villas were selling for – in some cases 30 per cent above fair market value. It also appeared that the sales commission included an 'advertising fee' of $30,000 per sale – which was up to 15 per cent of the purchase price!

Some time later, one villa owner rang my mate to talk about getting a revaluation for a potential sale. The valuer had to deliver the bad news that rather than increasing in value since his purchase of the unit for $200,000 three years earlier, it was now worth closer to $160,000.

The devastated owner informed the valuer that he had never seen the unit but bought it after a seminar by an 'investment adviser' who had co-ordinated the finance. It turns out the 'adviser' had also been the selling agent on the contract. The owner had cross-collateralised the investment loan with his own once-mortgage-free home in New South Wales. He was now at risk of losing both.

These tales are far too common. Ask questions to ensure your advisers are above board. In addition, seek out professionals who are members of industry bodies that require a code of conduct, such as PIPA.

## 4. Look for motivators

A great reason for building a dream team around you is that they can help break your investment paralysis and get you to step up, dive in and start paddling. Building the right team is a practical step towards making the big decisions.

I recently had a client who didn't build the right team, and the result was costly in terms of lost opportunities.

This client originally approached me in early 2017 but still seemed unsure as to whether he and his wife wanted to invest in property. They were in their mid-thirties, earning very good incomes, had about $500,000 in the bank in cash and were renting in Brisbane.

What a magnificent position to be in!

We ended up preparing a full plan for them, setting out a timeline for the strategy, and suggested they dip their toes in the water with a low buy-in property that was cashflow neutral, if not slightly positive. Despite us proffering two separate options in Hobart, they hit a wall in their decision-making process and, rather than bringing on a mortgage broker to help proceed with the program, asked us to hang fire so they could step back while they got comfortable with the decision.

I told them at the time, 'Look, I have to do what you want to do. I'm not going to push you to take on a mortgage broker but I think it would be a wise move. Come back to me when you're ready and we'll have another chat'.

It wasn't until June 2018 when they decided to join us once more. They'd saved another $40,000 in that time and were on even better incomes. The downside is that by not taking that first step of bringing a mortgage broker onto their dream team, they'd missed out on breaking their paralysis. I'd estimate the couple probably lost somewhere in the vicinity of $75,000 in capital growth that they would otherwise have achieved with the investment we initially suggested – and which was now at a positive cash flow.

And they were still of the same mindset as they had been more than a year ago, not wanting to jump in 'too quickly'.

I said, 'Well, it feels like you're never going to be 100 per cent certain of what to do, but let's reflect on what's happened in the past when you had cash, you had strong incomes and you still had the same reservations. We need to take some practical steps to get you in the market, and the first step is getting a mortgage broker on board'.

Fortunately, this time around, they acted and acquired a property by January 2019. No prizes for guessing what's happened since – one of the strongest capital gain periods in history from

2020 to early 2022 saw their wealth leap up. Even with the slow-down in value gains during the interest rate rises of 2022, they're still hundreds of thousands of dollars ahead in net wealth. What's great is that the latest data suggests there's more upside to come in the next few years too.

They moved forward and broke the paralysis cycle by ignoring the property naysayers in their lives and building a supportive network of professionals. Now, they're reaping huge rewards.

The job of a supportive dream team is to mobilise, activate and get things moving… because it's rare in property to hear someone say, 'I shouldn't have bought five years ago'. Most of the time, the biggest regret is, 'I should have bought when I could'.

## Where to find your dream team

As an investor, you will come to rely on a core stable of advisers to help light your way and lead you to success. Some will become lifelong advisers, while others may be project specific. It's not just industry professionals that you're looking for – family members or friends may well have useful skills, experience or attributes to add to the mix.

### Family and friends

I believe that we are the product of the five people we consider our closest allies. They cultivate our values, help set our motivations and even influence our attitudes.

If your nearest and dearest are already successfully investing in property, they should be your first port of call when you are seeking out property advisers.

Your family and friends will already have your best interests at heart, and some will have already found the diamonds in the rough. These are the sorts of advisers you want to hear from because you know their only bias when recommending a service provider is wanting to do what's best for you.

## Fellow investors

Beyond your own close-knit unit of kin and compadres are the fellow property investors you'll come across.

They may be people you've heard about and sought out. They could be parents of your kid's school friends. They might be workmates. They could even just be the folk who run the local corner store or deliver the mail.

They are people you run across who, through conversation about the mutually interesting topic of real estate, you realise are treading a similar path to your own. Ask about their experience with various advisers and see who they recommend.

## Forums and investment groups

Fortunately, we live in a well-connected world where those with common interests can gather and discuss their most pressing issues.

Take a look and you'll see that property investment groups are springing up everywhere. There are regular pub and café meet-ups as well as more formal get-togethers where moderators invite guest speakers to share their views.

Online communities are strong too. Forums such as propertychat.com.au offer a wealth of information on good and bad advisers. There's even the chance to connect with other investors through the comments section of more mainstream online publications too.

My proviso here is that as you begin forming relationships outside your trusted circle, remember to have a small dose of scepticism – nothing unhealthy, just an awareness that you must protect your own interests above all else.

## Online searches

'Hear, hear!' to the search engine.

It isn't that difficult to type in broad category keyword searches and come up with a list of local advisers who are all too eager for your business. You can even check out online reviews for them – although anonymous opinions on someone's performance can't always be trusted as they usually only tell half the story.

Another online source to watch is social media platforms. Most professionals post blogs and articles covering a broad range of subjects. If you read something you like, seek out the author and check if they are aligned with your goals and fit the dream team rules we've discussed in this chapter.

## Other advisers

In the field of property investing, success will lead to success.

If you find yourself with an excellent adviser – be it a mortgage broker, accountant, town planner or whoever – use their experience to find additional advisers in other fields. Most real estate accountants, for example, will have had dealings with solicitors specialising in property-related matters. Why not check out their recommendations?

The advantage here, apart from being able to rely on the advice of a professional you've already decided is worth your time and money, is that many will have an existing relationship with this other adviser. That usually makes for easier communication between them when needed, which is all a plus for you as the client.

## Chapter Hacks

- There's always more to learn about property, but apply a filter to give you a reality check.
- Select your dream team early.
- Look for dream team members with experience who are good communicators.
- When considering advisers, ask questions to ensure they are above board.
- Find people to motivate you, to help you be confident and decisive.
- Look around you (e.g. to family, friends, investment groups) as well as online for advisers.

# 6

# Building your dream team

We've talked in general terms about learning how to pick your dream team and why this is such an important step. Now it's time to home in on the detail.

There are three levels of dream team members:

1. **Non-negotiable** – your life partner, mortgage brokers, mentors, property investment advisers, buyer's agents.
2. **Second string** – solicitors/conveyancers, accountants, town planners.
3. **Reserve** – pre-purchase inspectors, equity partners/joint venture partners.

Let's take a look at the role of each in turn and work out why you need them.

## Non-negotiable dream team members

These are your key team members whose input is essential in helping you achieve your property investing goals.

## Your life partner

Your life partner is the most important member of your investment team.

In reality, this person is usually your co-captain, and without their support you might as well not be attempting to build a portfolio. Whether they be your husband, wife, de facto, girlfriend, boyfriend or any other significant other, your life partner plays an integral part in your success because of the nature of property investing.

Your life partner needs to be on board with your ultimate aims and the resources you have available to achieve them. They need to know how involved they are legally and financially. Will they be involved in co-ownership arrangements? Will the bank require them to sign over a mortgage or guarantee a loan? Do they agree with you about how many properties you'll buy, how much debt you'll carry and the level of risk the household should be taking on?

I've seen couples begin the journey toward creating wealth through property with one partner not ready to commit to the plan. This creates conflict and tension – sometimes just around the hypotheticals of what to buy and how much to risk. Imagine if these couples actually did buy something and hit a hurdle without having first discussed the processes in detail!

Another consideration, beyond the dollars and cents, is that your life partner is an essential cog in setting your barometer correctly. In fact, you will be aligning your dreams and ambitions. Make sure you both have the same goals and intentions when you commit to becoming landlords.

As you can probably tell from what I wrote in Chapter 1, without both Kim and I providing each other with the love and support needed to tackle the journey of real estate ownership, we could never have achieved what we have so far.

To paraphrase: happy life partner, happy life.

## Mortgage brokers

Your relationship with your mortgage broker is pivotal because, when all is said and done, property investing is about finance. Finance is a foundation stone for an investor because, in its basic form, it determines two primary factors: how much you can borrow and your financial tolerance for paying the loan back. The right mortgage broker can make or break a deal for their clients, which means they're crucial when you are building your portfolio.

The role of the broker is broadly to help you source the most appropriate finance for your property deals. They should be well-connected in the finance industry and able to field out your particular requirements to a reasonable-sized panel of potential lenders, seeking out those that offer the best terms for your deal. They should be independent of the lender and motivated only to work for you in landing the best possible finance arrangement.

While the term 'mortgage broker' can encompass a range of professionals able to help you source finance, not all brokers are the same. There are two important questions to ask a potential broker:

1. Do you specialise in helping people like me invest in property over the long term?
2. Do you invest in property too?

Some brokers try to be a jack-of-all-trades when it comes to sourcing finance for their clients, but the issues that affect property investors differ from those that affect homebuyers. For a start, the ever-dynamic lending landscape means interest rate movements, loan-to-value ratio limitations and risk assessments will vary depending on whether you are a homebuyer or investor, and also vary from one type of investor to another.

Modern history has helped forge exceptional professionals in this field, and it's those experienced specialists you should seek out. For example, in 2017, the Australian Prudential Regulation

Authority (APRA), the body that governs lending regulations for Australian institutions, brought in guidelines that meant banks had to slow the growth in their investor loans. The result was a raft of measures that made it tougher for investors to source finance, while owner-occupiers continued to get their loans approved. Mortgage brokers who operated under this lending regime and survived have come out with a wealth of experience that helps them take better care of their investor clients.

The second question, 'Do you invest in property too?', investigates whether your broker has the investor mindset themselves. It's even better if their strategies around real estate investing align with yours. They will have first-hand knowledge of the benefits and difficulties of sourcing finance for investors.

Your broker will help guide you through the finance application and approval process. I am not a broker, but after dealing with quite a few brokers professionally, I understand that their role relies on clients providing accurate and comprehensive information. You will need to provide as much information as you can on the following:

- **Incomes and outgoings** – from all income sources, not just your wage. Look at things like rental income, share dividends, bank interest earned, distributions from trusts, etc. Outgoings are your everyday expenses, as well as any monthly or annual commitments, such as mortgage repayments, school fees, vehicle running costs, etc.

- **Assets and liabilities** – sometimes referred to as your personal balance sheet. You should include all assets, from your house and car through to property and shareholdings, as well as major home furnishings and important jewellery items. Liabilities will comprise loans and other outstanding debts, particularly those secured by your assets.

## Mentors

For new investors, buying property to build wealth can seem like a daunting task, not least because the sector has its own language full of jargon, acronyms and abbreviations.

Here are some examples. You could be buying:

- a DA and BA approved site, or it could be STCA
- a double frontage block with twin gabled federation home including feature finials
- a medium density designated block with an above-average GFA yield due to the proximity of a designated neighbourhood centre.

Did you catch that? If you're new to the game, don't be too disheartened if the above reads like gibberish – there's a lot to learn (and a glossary at the back of this book!).

How handy would it be to have a smart property mind at your disposal to help you sort through this kind of terminology? Wouldn't it be great if you had someone experienced on hand to guide you through the wilderness as you build your own knowledge base about this real estate subculture and its tribes?

For exactly these sorts of reasons, having a decent property mentor is a must.

A property mentor can be anybody who is on board with your program of building wealth through real estate. Property mentors can be both paid and unpaid advisers who will help you along on your journey. They will be your champion, particularly when you hit the inevitable challenges that come with buying and selling property.

Some great mentors are as nearby as in your smart phone contacts list. Friends and relatives who've negotiated the dangers of the property jungle are fantastic. They are generally trustworthy, their advice is usually free and you can often reach them out of hours!

Mentors who are your friends and relatives are often excited about your success rather than envious. They are also likely to back you up when naysayers try to beat you down.

Imagine standing around at the next family barbeque when your less-than-motivated cousin starts doubting whether your scheme to build wealth through property will actually come off. Then your brilliant and well-travelled great aunt, who retired early on the back of her long-term property portfolio, steps up with a few choice words about her own success and how she applauds your gumption – it'll shut up that layabout cousin of yours in an instant!

Even if you don't have a close friend or relative who can be your mentor, fear not. Our property investing community is filled with members who are more than willing to lend a hand. As mentioned earlier, meet-up groups and online contacts can be excellent sources of information. Just make sure your mentor has a track record of their own success and isn't looking to sell you a service beyond great advice.

## Property investment advisers

The line between mentor and property investment adviser can be blurred, but for the purpose of our discussion, I'll differentiate them by assuming your property investment adviser will be paid for their services and advice, whereas your mentor probably will not be paid.

Property investment advisers are people like me who can be your holistic 'guide' as you ride the real estate surf. A great property investment adviser will have several key skills that set them apart.

First, they're great listeners. Each client's circumstances and desired outcomes are different. The number one skill these advisers need to possess is the ability to listen. Without total comprehension of what the investor wants to achieve, and the resources they have at their disposal, an adviser is flying blind when they give their advice and set a strategy. Make sure your adviser is listening, rather than just forcing their own opinion on you.

In many instances, a client knows they want something as simple as 'to retire by age 50', but that's the extent of their planning. A property investment adviser can tease out more details and work through the mental pathways that help set the new investor's personal barometer.

Second, advisers need to be investors themselves. As we've mentioned, there's nothing like having advisers who've 'walked the walk' with property. If your adviser has already dealt with the riptides and swells of property investing in their own lives, then they'll be well armed to defend you against the challenges and aim for the victories.

Third, they must be knowledgeable. Your adviser should be introducing you to concepts and strategies that make sense and challenge your thinking around property.

Finally, this is one dream team member with whom the lines of communication must be absolutely clear. You and your adviser have to be entirely open about all facets of your investing life. Whether they are delivering good or bad news, your adviser will make the outcome crystal clear. If a challenge to your strategy comes up, your adviser will help plot a clear path to overcome it. If you come away from a meeting with an adviser feeling overwhelmed and no better informed, then there's a problem – and it's not you, it's them. Advisers who can't talk your language are doing you a disservice.

A reminder again here that professional affiliations are a must in this field because, as at the time of writing, the property advisory industry is not subject to regulation. That's right – almost anyone can hang out a shingle and sell their services as a property adviser without any sort of regulatory oversight. It's scary stuff when you consider that we're talking about people spending hundreds of thousands, if not millions, of dollars on acquiring property.

Given this current unregulated environment, I'd strongly suggest you check whether the adviser you are considering is a member of PIPA. PIPA (Property Industry Professionals of Australia) is an industry group providing support and education for its members. In addition, it demands they adhere to a strict code of conduct to ensure they aren't operating illegally or unscrupulously.

Until such a time as comprehensive, legislated regulation kicks in to this industry, groups like PIPA are your best line of defence against unscrupulous operators.

## Buyer's agents

Again, the lines can be a bit fuzzy here, because buyer's agents can also be property investment advisers. In fact, using the one professional who combines these skills can be a huge bonus.

Buyer's agents are an absolute ace up the sleeve of real estate investors. The profession has really come of age in our country over the past decade. In the US, using an agent to buy property rather than just to sell it has been the norm for many decades, so it's refreshing to see wider acceptance by consumers of this valuable service in Australia these days.

The increased prominence of buyer's agents in the property industry can only be a good thing because they add a layer of professionalism to real estate deals. And it's logical – why shouldn't the buyer have a skilled professional representing their interests when seeking the best possible options for purchase?

Buyer's agents take care of a raft of challenges for their clients, including identifying the location, property type and price point that will fit their investment brief. Some buyer's agents even operate nationwide through a network of local contacts that can help pinpoint the best possible options for their clients.

There are other advantages too. Because buyer's agents constantly build and maintain their networks of agents and other professionals, they are often privy to deals that never make it onto listing portals. That's right, a buyer's agent can be part of off-market crackerjack investment deals that other potential purchasers won't even see.

In addition, and in my experience, selling agents like dealing with buyer's agents. When two parties are looking to lock down a contract, having an experienced professional agent representing both sides of the transaction helps open the lines of communication, smooths out the ambiguities and often results in a winning outcome.

You should try to find your buyer's agent in the same way you locate your other advisers, but I implore you to check their credentials and affiliations. Buyer's agents must be licensed to operate in the jurisdictions where they buy. In addition, buyer's agents should be members of groups such as the Real Estate Buyers Agents Association of Australia (REBAA) which insist that members follow a code of conduct.

## Second string members

While the teammates I've described so far form the core of your inner circle of advisers, there are others you'll come to rely on during your investment life. While they may not be on hand for ongoing, considered advice, these team members are still crucial to your success.

## Solicitors/conveyancers

Legal advice doesn't come cheap, but sourcing the mobile phone number of a smart, well-informed solicitor and conveyancer is essential when you're starting out.

You may not know that conveyancers don't always have to be lawyers, and specialist conveyancing firms do exist to help keep costs down in straightforward transactions. These sorts of organisations can be extremely useful and knowledgeable, but they won't be the right choice for every acquisition. A specialist property solicitor will be worth their fee when it comes to dealing with complex issues.

You don't have to use high-end legal firms to get great results. There are smaller companies that specialise in property conveyancing. These organisations will have intimate knowledge about dealing in property – and choosing a local operator can often be to your advantage.

If you have a question about adding or removing contract clauses, then your lawyer can help.

When you hit a hurdle in the process, where a seller is becoming toey about completing the deal, your solicitor will go in for the fight.

If you need advice on the best way to structure your purchase to protect your assets, it's probably time to meet with your solicitor.

Another important consideration when choosing your legal eagle is that your solicitor needs to be able to deal directly with your other dream team members – particularly your accountant and buyer's agent.

There will be circumstances when you're keen to minimise tax, or your long-term strategy includes avoiding paying a heap of stamp duty. This is when your solicitor will be able to provide the legal advice for the other property professionals on your team.

## Accountants

Rounding out your professional support suite is this key member of your gang.

Your accountant's main role is to save you money by minimising your taxes, avoiding unnecessary outlays and ensuring your strategy will see the most dollars land in your pocket (rather than the taxman's).

Finding an accountant who specialises in real estate is absolutely essential – and forming a relationship with one early in your investment journey is key. Accountants who know their numbers around bricks and mortar, and who can take a longterm view of your wealth building, can make sure you're purchasing property within the right tax structure (trust, company, individual or joint names).

In addition, there are strategies and loopholes that can help you minimise tax. For example, you may choose to live in a property before flipping it into your portfolio. How are things like the depreciable value of renovations likely to be viewed by the tax office? Will you need to live in a property for an extended period in order to take advantage of any CGT exemptions? How should your maintenance budget be treated to make sure you get the most possible back at the end of the financial year? Specialised accountants can help with all these challenges.

Accountants also come into their own when investors need to 'pivot'. If your well-thought-out long-term plans are upended by an unexpected wave, your accountant will help devise a financial strategy to make sure you aren't overly disadvantaged.

When seeking an accountant, be sure to lean on advice from your mentors – they will be right across who can best service your needs.

## Town planners

Whether you need a talented town planner on your team will depend on the stage you're at in your property investment journey.

If you are kicking off and looking for your first basic investment, which is high on cash flow, low on maintenance and reasonable on potential capital gains, then a town planner would be overkill. However, as you go past this initial foray into property investing and add a second, third or fourth property to your portfolio, the skills of a town planner become invaluable.

For example, say you're looking for a second investment – a house on land with a decent cash-flow position but some scope for very long-term redevelopment. By long-term, I mean at least 15 years down the track.

It's likely that you will be able to acquire such a property at a reasonable price because the higher-use potential is way off in the future. However, you want to make sure you acquire something with the right attributes for taking advantage of future urban growth.

A well-connected town planner will help you navigate local planning laws and will have insight into where the next location earmarked for higher densities might be. They might also have an opinion on what attributes to look for in a site, such as frontage, area and position in relation to transport and a commercial hub.

As you grow as an investor and take on more adventurous propositions, a town planner becomes essential.

Town planners will give you a 'heads up' early on about the potential your acquisition has for redevelopment, be it subdivision or construction. The more complex the deal, the more important a town planner becomes.

As you move into the realm of small development (more on this in Chapter 10), a town planner can actually help add tens of thousands of dollars to your bottom line, because they understand a hidden 'secret' not everyone is aware of: town plans are flexible. They are not hard and fast documents but, in reality, are a foundation upon which a talented town planner can build a profitable scenario.

Imagine you have a site that for all intents and purposes looks impossible to develop based on strict application of local area plan guidelines. Most punters would shrug their shoulders and walk away.

A town planner might look at that site and say, 'I know what the rules are, but with a few minor concessions to the council, I can put forward a plan that will make this property more valuable to its owners'.

Here's a case in point. I'm aware of a property in Brisbane that the owners had held for two decades. It was a decent size block of 790 sqm in one of the city's inner suburbs, but it was an awkward shape and drainage was an issue. While the owners were property valuers who knew their market, their interpretation of Brisbane's City Plan was that they couldn't split the site.

Fortunately, they employed a town planner to run a feasibility study of a subdivision.

While he confirmed that, yes, a strict reading of the plan showed no development would be possible, he was aware of some flexibility. He knew which section of council to meet with and was aware they were becoming proactive in increasing density in this suburb. Further, while the front boundary lacked width, he had successfully negotiated a similar style of project already where the position of the existing home made it possible to create a second access.

His assessment? He would meet with council on the owners' behalf and sell the benefits of the split to the local authority while making an allowance for setbacks.

The result? A tick from the local authority, very happy owners and a chance to create a new and very liveable space in a busy inner Brisbane suburb.

Winners all around.

## Reserve members

The final group of your dream team are like reserves on the bench. They are there for you to call upon should the need arise.

### Pre-purchase inspectors

You will find that from time to time you will need a variety of specialists to help you with a pre-purchase inspection. While these folks may not be on your long-term team, they act in your best interests come buying time, so it's good to know what they do.

Building and pest inspectors provide stop-gap insurance that can save you thousands of dollars. They will specialise within a specific location, so if you plan to make multiple purchases in one location, it's worth locking down a good one.

I've heard so many tales of property investors who've been saved by these unsung heroes. I know of an investor who found out via a diligent building inspector that the roof trusses in his new purchase were water damaged from a minor roof leak that had been dripping through over a very long time. It turns out that tiny flow had caused $10,000 of previously undetected damage. Fortunately, once the buyer made the seller aware of this situation, he was able to get the cost of these repairs knocked off the purchase price prior to settlement.

Pest inspectors unearth termite and white ant damage that others might miss. Once again, savings can be made by spotting the damage from these blighters early, and you may be able to include the repair or remediation costs as part of the contract conditions.

I'm aware of some investors who regularly use pest inspections as a negotiating tool as well. It works on the understanding that most properties will be exposed to white ants in some manner. One buyer I'm aware of always includes the pest clause in every contract with an expectation of using it to reduce the negotiated price. He specifically instructs the inspector to look for termite damage – even if the damage is to an old fence post that had been left lying in a garden bed near the back boundary away from the house. This buyer would then demand a reduction in the price for the cost of clearing the termites – regardless of whether or not the home had a barrier or was affected.

As a strategy, it's not a great one. It can create bad blood in the deal, and for buyer's agents who operate in specific areas it can result in a lousy reputation among their network of agents. You would have to make your own judgments on whether this is a 'good faith' way to negotiate, but it's not my idea of decent business practice.

This aside, having building and pest inspectors on board and ready to serve is a must if you're looking to mitigate risk in your next property purchase.

## Equity partners / joint venture partners

As you advance on your investment journey, you may look to take on more complex projects with more challenging elements. This means your dream team might evolve to include a joint venture (JV) partner or partners.

JV partners will become a part of your deals and will take on some of the risks in exchange for a share of the profits. Most commonly, they will share the responsibility of the finances in order to split profits, although I'm aware of some JV deals where a partner will contribute time and expertise instead of cash. There are even some project-managing buyer's agents who have arrangements whereby their clients provide all the funds for a venture while they project-manage the development to conclusion with a profit split at the end.

However the JV is divided, it can be a source of comfort and support for an investor, particularly if you've never attempted to take on a more complex venture, such as a speculative house construction or a small unit or townhouse project. The right JV partner can provide an enviable win-win for you both and it may lead to more projects in the future. That said, handing over part of the responsibility and profit to someone else requires a lot of planning and trust.

When it comes to JV partnership, here are my tips on what you must do.

**Make sure each contribution is equitable.** There are few things more frustrating in a JV than one partner doing all the hard work while the other seemingly looks on and waits for the profits. By 'equitable contribution' I don't mean you have to each grab the opposite end of the crosscut saw and start clearing the site of its towering gum trees. One partner might provide the money and the other might provide the skills. Just be certain you know, before you sign anything, what each other's responsibilities are and how your KPIs will be met.

**Be open, fair and honest.** You'll have probably picked up by now that I'm a keen proponent of communication – it's crucial to success in all your dealings. A JV partnership requires all stakeholders to be on board with a common goal. There can be no hidden agenda that might cause things to unravel. Similarly, you must be straightforward in what you can and can't bring to the table. It's all well and good for a partner to say 'I can handle the town planning aspects' in order to elevate their contribution to the project, but if they don't have the skills, understanding or time available to get this work completed properly then the whole deal could be in jeopardy. Be sure that if you say you're able to contribute something, you can and will do so. If you're having trouble holding up your end of the deal, speak up early.

**Source reliability.** A successful JV is a like a successful marriage. It's a relationship built on mutual trust and respect, where you both work toward a common goal and get to celebrate a beneficial outcome together. Choosing the right JV partner is crucial. If you can't select someone with a proven track record of JV successes, at least conduct a full due diligence on their previous solo investment and development dealings. Make sure you're not about to back a dud. Personal recommendations from trusted sources are always handy. One of the best ways to mitigate risk in this instance is to go with a professional buyer's agent or adviser who has built up a long-running and well-regarded business on the back of their skills as a JV partner.

**Always have a partnership agreement.** I honestly don't care if you're going into business with your twin sister who has held your hand from day dot – partnership agreements have saved marriages, family bonds and friendships. Partnership agreements are legally binding documents prepared by a suitably qualified professional which clearly outline the responsibilities and rewards for each member of the JV. They also include details around voting rights and conflict resolution.

Any financial arrangement – whether it be for a business, a building project or even a fundraising charity – will have some sort of agreement in place to address problems before they occur. As any smart solicitor will tell you, a partnership agreement is something you might never have to refer to during a successful venture, but it pays for itself many times over when you hit hurdles in the relationship.

This partnership agreement must address the unexpected too. What happens if illness or unemployment make it impossible for one of the partners to continue in the project? What if the project is midway through and there's already been a substantial overrun in time and money?

Partnership agreements will define the process of dealing with these situations. Everyone will know up front what to expect and how the money matters can be addressed.

**Make sure there is an exit strategy.** Finally, a partnership agreement around a JV must include an exit strategy. There needs to be a line drawn in the sand that defines when the deal is done, the agreement is over and the spoils have been distributed. This is important because you then have a common goal to strive towards, usually with a deadline and a definition of when the agreement ends. A sound exit strategy makes for a more effective and efficient relationship among JV partners, helping them work together to tick the list.

## Chapter Hacks

- There are three levels of members in your dream team: the non-negotiables, the second string members and the reserves.
- Your life partner is the most important member of your team.
- Each dream team member plays a vital role, some on an ongoing basis and others on a when-needed basis, depending where you are on your property journey.

# PART III
# PICKING THE RIGHT LINE

## 7

# Picking a location

It's time to get into the nitty gritty. We've talked about your hopes, dreams and aspirations. We've discussed the important elements of mindset and the essentials of preparation. We've defined the rules around building your dream team of advisers and support. Let's now look at what options await you as a real estate investor and how you can take advantage of each.

I love to travel the coastline and discover new and exciting surf spots where I'll be rewarded for taking the plunge. Something I've learned from this pursuit is that not all beaches perform the same way in the same weather conditions. As most wave riders know, different conditions create new opportunities to get wet at one break while other beaches go all 'lake-like'. A north-easterly may be blowing out the first open stretch of beach you spy, but head onto the other side of the peninsula, which is more protected by the prevailing winds, and you might find the swell direction is playing nicely off the point.

There are parallels between hunting for a perfect peak in surfing and picking the best property investment markets. You must read and understand the influences playing upon the markets and draw conclusions on the best place to stake your real estate claim.

## There's no one spot

I respect property professionals and their opinions about the markets; everyone has an opinion and they are rarely identical. As we've already discussed, humans have a natural tendency toward confirmation bias, so their position on the best place to buy real estate will vary depending on their own history and stimuli.

If you ask the nation's top 10 economists, 'Where's the best place right now for a property investment?', they will talk about jobs growth, unemployment rates and, potentially, price-to-income ratios. Now, this seems to be common sense: where there's the least unemployment, there are more people earning money and ultimately there is a growing economy – surely that's the recipe for growth?

However, it's just not that easy.

What I've learned from my years of investing is you can't look at single measures, like jobs growth, in isolation when assessing the investment viability of a location, nor can you just look at infrastructure spend by the local, state or federal governments. You can't only consider the unemployment rate and the level of private company investment either. The study of location selection is more complex than this.

The best illustration of how market peaks and troughs vary between locations that I've come across is a study completed by PIPA in 2018, which looked back our nation's capital city property cycles over 30 years. A 30-year timeframe will track some very serious periods of growth and retraction.

The original PIPA study was completed just after the Sydney price peak in 2017, so as you can imagine there was a whole generation of investors in the harbour city who had never seen a down market. In fact, many would have been looking towards other capitals such as Brisbane and Adelaide and wondering why any sane soul would invest there. Wasn't it obvious Sydney was the best place in Australia for extraordinary value gains?

To further illustrate the market evolution, I completed an analysis of the year 2017 to 2023 (the last of the tables coming up). This time of extraordinary upheaval included a global pandemic the likes of which we haven't seen since 1918.

Well, this entire study shows investors and homebuyers over the past three and a half decades have made solid returns across almost every capital city, depending on when they purchased.

For example, from 2003 to 2007, Sydney and Melbourne were Australia's worst performing capitals, despite being the best during the five years prior.

Turning to Brisbane, buyers who bought in 1988 saw the value of their asset double in less than five years, but by 1993 Brisbane was the nation's second-worst performing market.

Perth had an impressive five-year growth period with an increase in values of almost 140 per cent between 2003 and 2007 due to the mining boom, but throughout 2016–17 it was considered a real estate basket case.

Then there's Adelaide, which had languished in the shadows when it came to capital gains since the late 1980s. It dominated the numbers from 2017 to 2023.

A breakdown of findings makes for a compelling education.

## A cycle-by-cycle breakdown of Australian capitals

The tables overleaf show four- to five-year snapshots of the top performing cities for capital growth in the property market.

The assumption that any one location is always the best option for capital gains is false. There are opportunities to invest throughout Australia at different times. You just need the experience and resources to identify when to jump into a particular market.

| 1988 to 1992 | | |
|---|---|---|
| **Capital city** | **Increase** | **Ranking** |
| Brisbane | 99.0% | 1 |
| Sydney | 68.4% | 2 |
| Canberra | 66.8% | 3 |
| Perth | 56.7% | 4 |
| Hobart | 39.0% | 5 |
| Melbourne | 33.1% | 6 |
| Darwin | 32.8% | 7 |
| Adelaide | 25.2% | 8 |
| All capital cities (weighted average) | 55.8% | |

| 1993 to 1997 | | |
|---|---|---|
| **Capital city** | **Increase** | **Ranking** |
| Darwin | 56.5% | 1 |
| Melbourne | 20.6% | 2 |
| Sydney | 19.5% | 3 |
| Perth | 14.6% | 4 |
| Hobart | 6.9% | 5 |
| Adelaide | 4.3% | 6 |
| Brisbane | 3.8% | 7 |
| Canberra | -5.2% | 8 |
| All capital cities (weighted average) | 14.8% | |

| 1998 to 2002 | | |
|---|---|---|
| **Capital city** | **Increase** | **Ranking** |
| Melbourne | 88.2% | 1 |
| Sydney | 84.2% | 2 |
| Canberra | 60.1% | 3 |
| Adelaide | 60.1% | 4 |
| Brisbane | 48.1% | 5 |
| Perth | 41.6% | 6 |
| Hobart | 21.7% | 7 |
| Darwin | 5.1% | 8 |
| All capital cities (weighted average) | 70.0% | |

| 2003 to 2007 | | |
|---|---|---|
| **Capital city** | **Increase** | **Ranking** |
| Perth | 139.8% | 1 |
| Hobart | 126.4% | 2 |
| Darwin | 106.0% | 3 |
| Brisbane | 95.0% | 4 |
| Adelaide | 79.1% | 5 |
| Canberra | 60.0% | 6 |
| Melbourne | 59.9% | 7 |
| Sydney | 16.4% | 8 |
| All capital cities (weighted average) | 53.0% | |

| 2008 to 2012 | | |
|---|---|---|
| Capital city | Increase | Ranking |
| Darwin | 36.8% | 1 |
| Melbourne | 18.0% | 2 |
| Canberra | 15.0% | 3 |
| Sydney | 14.6% | 4 |
| Adelaide | 8.3% | 5 |
| Perth | 4.4% | 6 |
| Brisbane | 3.2% | 7 |
| Hobart | 1.9% | 8 |
| All capital cities (weighted average) | 12.2% | |

| 2013 to 2017 | | |
|---|---|---|
| Capital city | Increase | Ranking |
| Sydney | 74.6% | 1 |
| Melbourne | 63.7% | 2 |
| Hobart | 36.6% | 3 |
| Canberra | 26.9% | 4 |
| Brisbane | 25.1% | 5 |
| Adelaide | 21.7% | 6 |
| Perth | 0.6% | 7 |
| Darwin | -10.5% | 8 |
| All capital cities (weighted average) | 48.4% | |

| 2018 to 2023 | | |
|---|---|---|
| **Capital city** | **Increase** | **Ranking** |
| Adelaide | 61.1% | 1 |
| Brisbane | 54.4% | 2 |
| Canberra | 53.3% | 3 |
| Perth | 43.5% | 4 |
| Hobart | 40.7% | 5 |
| Darwin | 38.2% | 6 |
| Sydney | 53.3% | 7 |
| Melbourne | 25.6% | 8 |
| All capital cities (weighted average) | 46.2% | |

Sourced from Property Investment Professionals of Australia (PIPA)

## Four steps for picking location

So, given that choosing the best location is complex, and even experts disagree on this, what do I consider the best approach for choosing an investment location? I follow a four-step process.

### 1. Define your needs first

Before I begin, I keep in mind my basic investing philosophies as outlined in Chapter 2.

With my approach, I am going to be holding an investment for a minimum of 10 years (preferably 20 years), so I need to make sure I can afford where I buy and can service the debt over the long term. My financial resilience will determine how much I can invest, and this will in turn dictate where I can buy.

Sure, I still need to look at location and price in the context of what type of property investment I need in my portfolio at the time, but if I'm looking at it as a fundamental investment that's going to be a cornerstone property I hold for at least two decades, I want to be sure first and foremost that the property fits my budget – in terms of what I can afford to pay plus what I can afford to service and maintain during those 20 years.

Am I after a property that's going to give me good capital growth? Am I after something for cash flow? Am I after something I can develop? All of these are important considerations, but in the end my personal financials will set the bar of where I can buy.

## 2. Start big, end small

We live in a huge country and our options for investing are spread far and wide. After all, there are about 550 local authorities in Australia, and each contains multiple suburbs where markets are operating at different speeds.

So how do you filter through all that noise and select the right location for your portfolio?

The key is to start with the whole picture in mind and focus in until the answer reveals itself. Look from big region down to local authority, down to suburb, then down to street and individual property.

I'm happy to buy across a variety of locations, but most investors would only consider the capital cities and the biggest regional centres. This is reasonable given most of the property traded in Australia is located in the capital cities (around 60 per cent of volume nationwide is traded within Sydney and Melbourne) with the vast majority of remaining sales spread across 25 to 30 big regional centres.

With just a little effort through drawing on your own resources, including your dream team, you can get a fair idea of the data on our biggest centres. Looking at where these big population group-ings are in their market cycle will filter out a huge number and leave a handful that are showing promise of an eventual upswing.

The trick at this stage is to not analyse the data in so much detail you become paralysed by the process. Just define those regions where, in broad terms, the market appears due for value rises.

Once you've picked your best capital city or regional town, get right into the nitty gritty. You can reject those suburbs beyond your price range right away and then you'll be left with a few affordable suburbs.

The key here is to be realistic. Don't expect to find a sub-$500,000 detached home on 1,000 sqm, returning a yield of 7 per cent, within 4 km of Melbourne's CBD. You are wasting your effort and exhausting your enthusiasm.

It would be best to look at median house prices across your suburb list. Noting the distance from the CBD will help separate the wheat from the chaff because, as a very general rule-of-thumb, the further out a suburb sits, the lower the median price.

Once you use these parameters to isolate your suburb list, then get into the detail, picking over every listing and checking compa-rable sales to see which location will offer the best opportunities. Refine your choices along the lines of median price point, median rental yield and property type to make sense of the puzzle.

This macro to micro approach filters out the white noise and can help you quickly find the best locations for your investment.

### 3. Use all the metrics

There are a number of key measures you must look at when ana-lysing a market – and the way they interact tells a story.

Say I'm looking at a location from a rental strength perspec-tive. Typically, a sub-2.5 per cent vacancy rate that's trending down is a positive sign ... but it's not the whole story.

Hobart in 2018 was a great example. If you'd looked at Hobart in 2016, there was a distinct lack of housing supply, but the economy was a basket case, so demand was in equilibrium. In fact, the population had been going backwards as residents left for the mainland looking for work. This meant that there was no new construction as the existing housing supply was taking care of current demand.

Well, this is exactly when my company thought Hobart presented an excellent opportunity for investment. My team knew that counter-cyclical buying and the ability to look beyond today's bad data meant we'd discovered a window of opportunity. There was plenty of information – some highly qualitative – that indicated Hobart was due for an upswing. We placed a heap of clients into that great southern capital from 2016 onwards, using our own interpretations for wider data and applying our own unique forecasting measures… and guess what? The city saw extraordinary value growth of over 50 per cent from 2015 to 2018.

With a change of government, Tasmania's economy began to improve and job opportunities followed. This brought people to the Apple Isle, who were starting to demand housing in an economy where construction had pretty much stalled.

What happened? Vacancy rates trended even lower, rents rose and the value of property increased. There was more demand for new construction, and this, in and of itself, helped create more jobs.

Hobart had come off a low base, so the gains were pretty spectacular. That said, anyone who'd been looking to purchase in Hobart in 2016 who wasn't watching trends across all the interrelated measures of population growth, economic gains, housing supply and rental vacancy wouldn't have seen what was in store.

Best of all for those who did invest, it only continued to strengthen. The pandemic resulted in a heap of Australians looking to be isolated in beautiful Tasmania. They could work remotely or even retire to a nice home for a fraction of what it cost in Sydney or Melbourne.

But the primary lesson is this – no one metric tells the whole story. Study your district's data and think about the cause and effect when one metric plays off against another. It's only then you gain a comprehensive understanding of a region's potential.

### 4. Stay current

When you're on the hunt for a location, recent information is the best information.

There is no use drawing on dated data because markets shift, and you could be relying on figures that indicate a market is on the rise when, in fact, it is falling.

Also, ensure your data source is reliable. Look at how the information and results are collated so you can track the trends, and see if there are predictable outcomes that you may be able to foresee.

I suggest you use only one data source for each of your measures (I tend to primarily rely on CoreLogic). The reason is all big data houses have their own methods of calculating metrics. For instance, 'auction clearance rate' will mean something different depending on who you ask. The parameters CoreLogic uses to measure median house prices will differ from those used by SQM Research. It's impossible to accurately track the trends if you switch from one data source to another because the way they apply their analysis will vary.

Finally, stay on top of your research. It takes effort but pays dividends. In my business, we force ourselves into a deep dive of locational analysis every three months, without fail. One person takes charge at that quarterly meeting and allocates responsibilities for each person within our buyer's agency team – myself included – to research the numbers. The intention is that we'll pick up three to four new markets we haven't discussed before. It's also a chance to revisit our opinions on the regional analysis we've been doing. We go through a full list of locations and identify which need further research, and make sure everyone is on board with our decision-making.

Out of that exercise, we typically make a collective decision as a business to identify markets we should be in, those we should be leaving and those that are not quite ready for investment. We think about what types of properties our clients need for their portfolios and how these locations best meet their requirements.

There will always be tweaks and changes worth monitoring in property markets. Legislative rules will vary, new economic drivers will appear and town plans will alter.

It sounds complex and time-consuming, but when you are selecting locations it's important that you are well informed and stay current, because your judgement is being backed by hundreds of thousands of dollars of hard-earned money.

## Chapter Hacks

- It's difficult for experts to agree on top locations, and that's because there is no one spot.
- Property value growth is cyclical in each capital city location.
- We've tried and tested a four-step process of choosing where to invest:
  1. define your needs
  2. start big, end small
  3. use the metrics
  4. stay current.

# 8

# Understanding investment types

Every surfer has their favourite break. There's no doubt we find our comfort zone and become familiar with the lay of our preferred spot. It usually means we can get the best out of any conditions there. If it's a point break, where the non-locals are making a long paddle from the beach, we're probably the crew you see leaping from the boulders and using knowledge of the 'key' to enter from the rocky peninsula, so we can safely dive in and make a short paddle to the take-off zone. If we love a particularly open beach, we'll be aware of how the sand banks move and usually know which pockets help form the most solid walls.

The terrific thing about surfing is it's a sport that demands the participant to continually challenge themselves in order to improve their skills. There's no point paddling around in the white water indefinitely – the fun is out the back!

It's the same with property investing. You'll start off with some simple guidelines and then move forward into more complex, potentially riskier but increasingly rewarding ventures that fit your strategy and your barometer.

We'll discuss later how investors evolve (that's in Part IV). First, it's useful to outline the options available to you in today's property market. I'll then reveal the secret of how best to use these investment types to maximise the results of your portfolio over the very long term.

## Cash-flow investing

There's an old adage favoured by the crustier members of business that claims, 'Cash flow is king'. In many respects, this is true, but it doesn't tell the whole story.

The importance of concentrating on cash flow when you are investing really cannot be overstated, because a strong cash flow is what keeps you afloat as an investor – particularly over the long term.

One of my associates is known to say, 'No one ever went broke in real estate because their equity went backwards'. Property investors secure their holdings by applying to a financier, locking in loan terms and then dealing with the repayments over a number of years that often stretch into decades. In almost all cases, the financier will not be conducting a yearly audit of your property's value to determine if it has fallen. They're not concerned with watching the short-term increases and downturns in your property's value. They are unlikely to run screaming, hair on fire, to their credit department to call in the loan because your capital position has dropped a few per cent.

However, miss a few loan repayments and see how quickly you start to get your lender's undivided attention.

While most people build property wealth through long-term capital gains, there's no doubting cash flow is what keeps your head above water while you wait for the long-term market to do its thing.

## What is cash-flow positive?

Put simply, a cash-flow-positive property is an investment where the annual rental income covers all yearly costs, from mortgage repayments to maintenance to council rates, property management fees and charges – the lot – and there are some dollars left over that go straight back into your bank account.

Cash-flow-positive zealots take this further. They use this extra money each month to prop up more borrowings that are leveraged into another cash-flow-positive property, which generates additional net income for you – and so on, and so on.

Can you see where this is heading? This aim of this model is to build up a portfolio so big that the total combined net leftover income equals your wished-for retirement income. Simple!

Well, not really – read on to see where the dangers lie.

## Is cash flow important?

The short answer, as we've already established, is yes: cash flow is important. Paying attention to cash flow is key when you are building wealth because as you continue to extend yourself and acquire further holdings, your monthly loan commitments need to be met. If you plough into a pure capital gains strategy without any thought as to how you are going to service your loans, you will not last.

I had a discussion with a colleague recently that highlighted the importance of cash flow.

He's a property valuer and spoke about his dad – an ex-real estate agent and financier – who lived with some regret that he had never acquired a Brisbane riverfront block of land back in the early 1980s for the princely sum of $250,000. In 2007, the same block of land had been relisted with price expectations close to $3 million, and I suspect in 2023 dollars the value would be much closer to $9 million.

But as my mate and I worked through the numbers, it became obvious. The price of the site was already well over 10 times his dad's annual wage in the 1980s. But perhaps more importantly, it was vacant, so it was not generating a rental income. Even as a professional earning a relatively strong income, my mate's father wouldn't have been able to service the loan, because this sort of investment was a pure capital growth play – there was no cash flow help from a tenant.

Had my mate's father acquired this property, his funds would have drained away, particularly as he headed into a period of ever-increasing interest rates in the late 1980s. He would have gone broke and been scrambling to cover the loss. The lack of cash flow would have meant he wouldn't have had enough time to stay in the market and let the property's value skyrocket.

Properties with high cash flow help their landlords rest easy. They offer an income buffer so the owners are comfortable that no matter what else happens in their lives, their cash-flow-heavy investment will continue to 'wash its own face' financially.

## The dangers of cash flow

The theory behind buying property just for cash flow may appear sound on the surface – and it's an approach sold to many novice investors as a winning strategy for building wealth.

But here's why investing in cash-flow-heavy property alone can be your undoing.

First, as you won't be getting much capital growth you'll have to buy a bigger number of properties to achieve similar returns in the form of cash flows. Having excessive borrowings is risky – particularly if you're in a location where capital growth isn't assured. Ask anyone who borrowed to their absolute limit in late 2021 expecting interest rates to remain at historic lows. Just a few months later the upward hike of rates began, and by early

2023 they'd ballooned from 0.1 per cent to 4.1 per cent. That's a 41-fold increase! If you've overextended yourself on a loan and are running at the absolute limits of your income, then there's almost no chance you can service such a hike in repayments.

Also, cash flow investments tend to trade off that high income against their capital gains potential. In other words, you could feasibly be buying properties that will hardly see any increase in value over the long term. This sounds fine if you're looking to replace an income, but the real dollars in wealth creation are made in capital gains, not cash flow.

Worst of all, locations where you find all the cash-flow-heavy properties, as a broad rule, have less potential to maintain property values. If the value of your property goes backwards, you could be paying off a loan that actually exceeds your property's value.

One last word of warning: remember that rents can drop. The expectation that a location's rental demand will continue to rise and drive up your rental income is foolish.

For an example of these problems at play, you only need to look at Moranbah in 2007. The mining boom in Queensland was unprecedented, and Moranbah was the poster-child 'coal rush' town for property investors.

There simply wasn't enough accommodation in Moranbah to house all the workers employed by massive mining projects. There was plenty of money being splashed around to entice them away from the cities and into the regions.

Things were so good that some tenants even took up the practice of 'hot bedding', whereby a day-shift worker and a night-shift worker would actually rent the same bed! That's right – they'd pass each other every morning and evening as one headed off to the giant coal hole while the other hit the hay. (Hopefully changing the sheets after each sleep shift was part of the arrangement.)

And so, the investors were flocking in with dollar signs in their eyes, keen to take a huge slice of the cash-flow pie in Moranbah. I'm aware of at least one medical professional (so, a very smart guy) who, at Moranbah's market peak, paid over $900,000 for a property that was generating $1,300 per week in rental income. That's a gross yield of 7.5 per cent – not bad.

But the good times were never going to last forever. The eventual mining boom fallout saw operations fold and the workforce leave.

By 2016, the Moranbah market was a shell of its former self, with vacancies rising and property values plummeting. The medico's house sat vacant; he was unable to get a tenant at $300 per week, and the updated bank valuation of the property came in at $350,000.

Putting all your eggs in the one cash-flow basket can be tempting, but good sense and knowledge about the cyclical nature of real estate dictates you should diversify your investments.

My earnest suggestion to those considering a cash-flow-only portfolio is this: don't hang your hat on this one measure of return. Look for the fundamentals that help mitigate the risks – for example, look for multiple industries that are helping drive the local economy, or a tightening or control of future housing supply.

Make sure you understand what is driving the market and whether it's susceptible to fall before you commit to cash-flow-positive property.

## Can I improve my cash flow?

Unearthing cost-effective ways to boost your investment's cash flow is satisfying and smart. There is a number of strategies you can use to help improve your rental income. Here are two popular options we've explored.

One simple method to increase cash flow is to improve the appearance or layout of your property through **renovation and reconfiguration** so it's more appealing to tenants.

The work could be cosmetic. A couple of coats of paint and paying some attention to the streetscape will set your property above the rest.

Another strategy is to create more accommodation options. If you find a property in a university catchment zone, for example, some local councils will allow you to rent it out to numerous students on multiple by-the-room tenancies – so long as you comply with building and accommodation codes. Could your holding's downstairs area be converted into three bedrooms, a communal kitchen and adequate bathroom facilities for multiple tenants? If it could, then the result could be hundreds of dollars more each week in rental return.

It's a savvy strategy, but not one you should venture into without relying on the advice of professionals to make sure you select the right property and comply with building requirements and the relevant planning codes.

Another way to boost your cash-flow returns is to create an additional dwelling on your allotment by constructing a secondary home, which is usually self-contained. These are known as 'ancillary dwellings', or, more commonly, 'granny flats'.

As with the student-style accommodation strategy, the building and renting out of an ancillary dwelling is subject to a raft of local government legislation and building compliance, but it can be a lucrative strategy if your property and the market fit the criteria.

Over the past decade, plenty of buyer's agents have sprung up who will locate properties with the potential for an ancillary dwelling on your behalf. This reduces the time it takes to source one of these cash-cow investments. And there is no shortage of property investors looking to buy existing, council-approved, dual-income-style properties, so you do have a reasonable pool of potential buyers when the time comes to sell.

In 2012, I sourced a property in southwest Sydney for a client, which came with potential but also some challenges. It was a small, fibro, three-bedroom house on a corner block of around 550 sqm, and there was potential to add a two-bedroom granny flat.

We were somewhat pioneers in this strategy at the time. The local area plan had only recently been changed to allow granny flats on these smaller blocks, so we were one of the first to give it a go. This was a blessing and a curse, because we were testing the market without the benefit of other recent comparable sales to use in our due diligence. The upside was that by getting into the game early, we could acquire the site and complete the project with less competition, which meant we were in a better position to negotiate the price at which to buy the 'parent' holding.

It took four months for us to complete the build of the ancillary dwelling and we got a tenant straightaway. In addition, the existing tenant in the 'parent' house was aware we were about to start a build and had agreed to sign a fixed lease, which secured our cash flow during the project.

In the end, we had an investment yielding 9 per cent gross, which is pretty handy for a cash-flow purchase.

The biggest downside we hit was that because there were so few properties like this in the area, the initial valuation we got wasn't up to scratch. A lack of comparable evidence meant the valuer came up with a figure based entirely on the detached houses in the surrounding area – and none of these were generating as much cash flow as ours.

So, we waited… and in 2023, a revaluation proved we'd made the right move as the property had increased in value by almost three and half times the original purchase price.

Here's the breakdown of the project from back then as compared to now:

**2012**

| | |
|---|---|
| Purchase price: | $250,000 |
| Cost to build the granny flat: | $100,000 |

**2023**

| | |
|---|---|
| Rental income: | House: $460 per week |
| | Granny flat: $415 per week |
| Gross yield on outlay: | Over 13 per cent |
| Revaluation: | $850,000 |

The secret? Patience. But we couldn't have been successful without the cash flow. We had a secure rental income, which gave us time to let the market do its thing without having to sweat about where the next mortgage payment would come from.

## Capital growth

You don't have to travel far into the world of real estate investment before you stumble upon devotees of the capital growth approach to property investment.

To be frank, just about everyone who has built serious wealth for their future has done so by generating capital gains when building their real estate portfolio.

### What is capital growth?

While it may seem like overkill to go through it, properly understanding the definition of capital growth is essential if you want to make the correct decision on where to invest your dollars.

Capital growth (or capital gains) refers to the increase in value of your asset over time. You'll often see capital growth expressed as either a percentage or dollar amount stated alongside the period over which it improves (or, in the case of some mining towns, falls).

For example, if you have $500,000 to invest and you achieve a capital gain of 5 per cent in the first year, then your property will be worth $525,000 at the end of year one. I suppose that sounds like easy money – you do nothing and realise $25,000.

Well, it's a little more complex than that, as we'll discover later in this chapter.

For now, just remember that knowing how much a property's value has risen, and over what timeframe, is critical in understanding what makes for a good investment and what doesn't.

## What determines capital growth?

The elements that drive capital growth and property values sit squarely within the foundations of economics, and they are the two measures on which entire societies operate and survive: supply and demand. Basically, if the demand for an asset exceeds the supply of that asset, then its price will rise. Conversely, if there's little demand for the asset and plenty of supply, its price will fall.

A great property example of this relationship can be found in one of my favourite capital cities. The inner-city, high-rise unit market in Brisbane from around 2013 to 2018 should be considered a textbook case of how markets ebb and flow from extremes to equilibrium.

Brisbane's relative affordability, the low cost of living and myriad other benefits provided the hallmarks of a great option for developers looking to profit in 2013. There was also excellent demand from overseas investors (particularly from Chinese investors) looking to bolthole cash in a new product.

Throughout 2013 to 2015, there was an absolute troupe of cranes dancing across the city skyline – particularly in South

Brisbane and West End, where one-bedroom investor stock couldn't be built fast enough. Off-the-plan buying was hot, and many buyers were barely checking over the floor plans before they put down a deposit.

Demand from investors for new product was high and supply was initially low, so the equation worked in favour of developers keen to make a quid.

Unfortunately, the overshoot of unit supply was bound to come. From mid 2016 to early 2017 there were enough planned and recently completed projects within central Brisbane to cater for 15 years of average demand – and many of the new developments were due to be completed within 12 months of each other. That means if you added together all the new unit stock that was available for sale and the number of units being constructed, and then included the number that had received planning approval, Brisbane City Council could have raised the drawbridge and happily accommodated the average annual level of demand for units for the next decade and a half. Supply was at a record high.

Soon after, a convergence of factors came into play that gutted demand. Financiers started to tighten the lending criteria on investor loans, while political moves were made to restrict foreign investment. Suddenly a whole raft of potentially profitable unit projects found themselves to be like real estate wallflowers at a school social dance: no one was interested in them.

There are no prizes for working out what happened next.

Valuers I have spoken to say revaluation of many of these inner-city investments, from the time they were purchased to the time they were completed, saw a drop in value of up to 20 per cent from their original contract price. That means there are people who contracted to buy an off-the-plan unit for $450,000 and, for that privilege, just a couple of years later are faced with the prospect of being handed an asset worth $360,000.

It's a classic case of high supply, low demand... you get the idea.

Of course, the price boom of 2021 coupled with today's incredibly tight rental market means much of this oversupply had been absorbed by 2023 – but I guarantee those unit investors haven't achieved as much capital gain as detached homeowners over the same time period. That's a discussion around 'opportunity cost', which we'll cover later.

## Basic growth drivers

So what are the factors that help push the 'demand' side of the equation in your favour as an investor? What are the things you need to look for in a location, property type or price point that will help drive price rises in the future?

Locations with **a diverse economic base** are appealing because when one part of the economy is softening, there are other parts still helping to drive employment, wage growth and the flow of money. This leads directly to increased demand.

Single-industry locations, such as regional mining towns, are tethered to the success of one major employment type. If that starts to sink (for example, if a resource price drops) there will be a whole heap of trouble for the local wage earners.

This is why many investors consider capital cities to be more reliable investment locations than smaller regional centres. For novice investors in particular, it's hard to imagine Sydney, Melbourne or Brisbane 'failing' on a grand scale when there are so many options for wage earners.

One part of a robust local economy is the ability to look after its citizens. The quality of fundamental **services, facilities and infrastructure** make potential investment suburbs fairly easy to spot.

The presence of good schools, shopping and medical facilities are a no-brainer. When you have these on offer in a location, the convenience of holding a property in reasonable proximity is awesome.

Another key element is the ease in which residents can move around. Transport infrastructure is an excellent measure of possible value gains, like new rail extensions that bring outer suburbs closer to the CBD via shorter travel times. Dedicated busways also ensure an easier commute. Thoughtful road projects designed to reduce travel time and ease gridlock are all on an investor's list of must-haves.

While many of these tick-list items can be city-wide initiatives, localising them helps one suburb outperform its neighbours. When the Sydney city light rail project got the green light, property in some lesser well-known addresses enjoyed a huge boost in value as both businesses and residents weighed up the convenience of buying away from higher profile, more expensive locations.

Lifestyle is also a big influencer as it flows on from services, facilities and infrastructure. Now I'm not suggesting that weather is a major influencer of capital gains (although it is to some extent if you're pitching to the retiree market, I guess), but people want to be happy with where they choose to live.

Parks, community sporting facilities, safety and security – these are all attributes that make any location a desirable place to live. Don't discount their ability to help push prices up when you're looking at where to invest your dollars.

Think of some of the inner-city suburbs in Sydney that a couple of decades ago were no-go zones for safety. Redfern is an excellent example. Entire episodes of tabloid television were devoted to the social challenges facing this postcode, but try to buy a detached home there now and you'll be competing with high-income professionals and trust fund recipients.

**Scarcity** is a fundamental supply driver that helps investments continue to rise in value.

Why do you think our high-end, ultra-prestige Sydney waterfront addresses seem to continue to increase in value unabated? Because, to paraphrase the old adage, 'they just aren't making any more waterfront land'. There is only so much high-quality stock where the waters lap against your private dock, so any buyers with the financial means to acquire one of these homes must fight for what's available.

Sure, everything has its price, but if you're hankering for a jetty running off a large lawn in the shadow of a three-level mansion then your options are limited.

Of course, this example is extreme. Scarcity applies to more humble locations as well. A detached home on 800-plus sqm within 4 km of any of Australia's major cities is a rare commodity, so expect the price of these asssets to be firm over the long term too.

Ramp up the scarcity factors and you ramp up the value. Imagine a house close to the city, add rare views of the city, and it becomes even more costly. Make it a beautiful colonial style or one-off contemporary architect designed home on a flat block with a wide frontage... you get where I'm going with this. All of these attributes help increase the scarcity factor, which is a direct limit on supply, which then sees the value of these properties stay strong.

## The magical world of compound growth

Gaining skill in a particular discipline takes time and consistent effort. When I started surfing at a very young age, I began on the beach learning how to position myself on a board and practising how to get to my feet in one fluid motion. I would practise this until I was tired and sore, but eventually the muscle memory kicked in and I could make the leap without thinking.

Then, it was into the white water, where I learned about how the waves moved. I would study sweeps and rips and think about how to paddle through the wash. I learned through catching the white water and getting to my feet until board rash kicked in or the sun was about to set. Practice, practice, practice.

Then I went out beyond the break, studying how wave sets come in and when was the best time to hammer down and paddle until you couldn't lift your arms any more but were safely beyond the break. I learned about positioning myself so for minimum effort I could push onto a wave and make the drop. Each step was a small challenge I had to overcome until it no longer took a great effort. Each time I was building upon skills and setting a new benchmark for success.

Time and effort are necessary to learn anything worthwhile. The ability to make an effort, reap a reward and build upon success to reach greater heights will result in you achieving goals you might have once thought impossible. The same logic can be applied to capital growth investing, and it's why it attracts so many devotees.

The primary reason capital growth investing is considered an exceptional approach to maximising your wealth is that you are building on your success to grow your results. This is the basis of compound growth – and like training for a physical challenge, this financial strategy is realised best over time.

With compound growth, instead of taking out any value gains from your investment, you leave them in your asset so they can help build value even further. What you find is that your investments improve in value exponentially over time – and the longer you leave it, the better the growth.

## An example of compound growth

Let's take our example from earlier and go a little further with it, to demonstrate.

Say you invest $500,000 in a property in a growth location that will see values improve by 5 per cent per year on average. That means in year one, your asset improves in value by $25,000 to $525,000.

Not too bad!

You decide to hold onto this asset at its new value of $525,000 rather than selling down, taking the money and running – thus you are effectively reinvesting this capital gain back into the market. This means in year two, at 5 per cent growth, your asset now worth $525,000 will go up in value by $26,250 and be worth $551,250, which you will once again roll over into the market simply by choosing not to sell.

Do you see where this is going? By choosing not to sell, compound growth means that your initial $500,000 property will be worth closer to $750,000 in 10 years' time. Hold on for 20 years under these parameters and you'll find yourself with a property worth over $1.325 million in your portfolio.

The table opposite shows how a compounding growth asset outperforms a non-compounding investment over a 20-year period.

Now, imagine applying this to multiple properties in a structured portfolio. You eventually start seeing your holdings grow by more each year than you could earn as a wage. This is where your goal to live your best life suddenly becomes a reality, because you get to choose how to spend your time.

You can see why the idea of capital gains are so attractive to investors. The growth potential is monster!

| Asset value purchased for $500,000 with a 5% p.a. value growth | | |
|---|---|---|
| Year | Value not compounded | Value compounded |
| 0 | $500,000 | $500,000 |
| 1 | $525,000 | $525,000 |
| 2 | $550,000 | $551,250 |
| 3 | $575,000 | $578,813 |
| 4 | $600,000 | $607,753 |
| 5 | $625,000 | $638,141 |
| 6 | $650,000 | $670,048 |
| 7 | $675,000 | $703,550 |
| 8 | $700,000 | $738,728 |
| 9 | $725,000 | $775,664 |
| 10 | $750,000 | $814,447 |
| 11 | $775,000 | $855,170 |
| 12 | $800,000 | $897,928 |
| 13 | $825,000 | $942,825 |
| 14 | $850,000 | $989,966 |
| 15 | $875,000 | $1,039,464 |
| 16 | $900,000 | $1,091,437 |
| 17 | $925,000 | $1,146,009 |
| 18 | $950,000 | $1,203,310 |
| 19 | $975,000 | $1,263,475 |
| 20 | $1,000,000 | $1,326,649 |

As I mentioned back in Chapter 1, it's all about where you start. Adopting a capital growth strategy to take advantage of compound growth relies on a couple of well-chosen strategic investments to start with. These set the groundwork for future gains. Get these right and you'll be looking good.

The other great thing about capital growth investments is that as a set-and-forget (within reason) strategy, they yield a big outcome for little input. If you can build a $2 million portfolio of capital growth assets that are rising by a very modest 5 per cent per annum, then your wealth is increasing by $100,000 in year one – with the magic of compounding yet to follow. That's a pretty decent 'wage', don't you think?

Capital growth is also often low yielding, so if you're looking to take advantage of negative gearing benefits, then high-growth assets will feature heavily among your holdings. That said, I don't think tax benefits should ever be your primary motivation for investing. They are always a sweetener, but for growth investors there is more opportunity in taking advantage of compounding.

## The risks of capital growth investing

So, why doesn't everyone just get into blue-chip, high-growth assets and wait for their chance to become mega-millionaires? Because servicing the loans on a high-debt, low-yield portfolio can be tough, with plenty of risk for those who are unprepared.

As we've already discussed, no one goes broke in property from a loss of equity – it's the drying up of cash flow the financiers care about most.

As a gross generalisation, most assets are viewed as either high growth or high return. So, while you might be enjoying growth in value of your assets on your balance sheet, the bank also wants you to generate adequate cash flow to cover the monthly repayments.

Over-leveraged borrowers who acquire multiple low-yield properties place themselves under severe financial strain. Any hiccough in the timeline – such as job loss or an interest rate rise – can result in the bank asking questions as to why they aren't being paid on time.

I am a champion of capital growth investing, but you must be smart about it. You should never risk your financial health or the wellbeing of your family by biting off more than you can chew. This is why it's a must to have a talented, independent mortgage broker and property investment adviser by your side. (Remember your dream team?) Your broker will help keep you out of strife, while your investment adviser will help you pick the best assets for your budget.

## Cash flow versus capital growth

Anyone who has studied property investment for a long time will have come across this old chestnut of a debate: cash flow versus capital growth. It's terrific to watch experts intellectually cage fight about this seemingly innocuous five-word riddle, as there's often passionate argument from both sides.

I'm going to throw my hat in the ring – what do I think about cash flow versus capital growth?

We now know cash flow helps us offset the monthly costs of our holdings, but high cash flow carries risks that can see us miss out on big returns in a turning market, and there's traditionally less exponential growth in your net wealth.

On the other hand, high-growth assets see your personal wealth increase exponentially, but loan servicing costs can drive you to the financial brink.

What's the solution? In my opinion, it's balance and diversification that matter.

## Finding equilibrium

If you choose one strategy to the exclusion of the other, you're bound to hit a roadblock on your investment journey – so try to achieve a healthy mix of both.

Let's take a look at the actual numbers that show why ignoring this approach causes so many people fail to build a substantial portfolio. In round figures, approximately 70 per cent of Australia's investment properties are negatively geared (see the next section), but approximately 75 per cent of investors with negatively geared properties have a taxable income of $80,000 or less. In addition, 80 per cent of property investors own only one or two investment properties and stop there.

Based on these statistics, it appears most median-income investors are buying properties that are losing cash flow over the long term while they wait for an appreciation in value so they can re-invest the equity. The result seems to be that they become worn down by not having better cash flow and give up on investing after just one or two holdings.

I know we continually read that you should always invest for capital growth rather than neutral or positive cash flow, which is 'lazy investing'. Don't get me wrong, plenty of investors (including me) have made significant capital gains by investing in holdings in high-growth areas that offer yields of 4 to 5 per cent but have a negative cash flow. My point is that these types of properties shouldn't be your first or second purchase. Instead, build a solid foundation of growth plus cash-flow holdings first. Sure, you might forgo an 8 per cent growth opportunity and instead acquire a 6 per cent yielding investment in a 5 per cent growth zone, but the financial buffer it creates allows you to hold for longer and enjoy the benefits more comfortably – particularly if you're a lower income earner wanting to build a portfolio of more than one property. How will the bank approve funds if you buy a $500,000 property at only 3 per cent yield and with no substantial back-up source of income?

It's important that investors don't 'invest themselves out of the market' through selecting negative-cash-flow properties early on in their journey. You should always consider your current portfolio, position, income, dependants and financial and investment goals to determine what your next investment should be – whether that is a high-growth property or cash-flow-positive property or a blend of both. The type of investment property you choose should always serve a purpose in achieving your investment goals.

In the end, it will be your long-term plans that will help you decide which property to invest in.

## Negative gearing

The debate on the various benefits and implications of negative gearing has been raging for as long as tax has been an election issue – which has been ages.

For those who don't understand the concept, negative gearing allows landlords to boost their after-tax income by claiming as a deduction the net loss in income that results from holding their investment property. So, if your investment property earned you $20,000 per year in rent, but the total claimable costs of repairs, maintenance, fees, rates, statutory changes and bank interest came to $25,000, you would have a $5,000 loss you could include in your personal tax return.

Some property investment schemes rely on this strategy, convincing landlords they should adopt a 'negative cash flow' approach to alleviate their tax burden while the value of their holding skyrockets. Here's my opinion on that particular approach – it's ridiculous!

Negative gearing should never be relied on to direct you into a specific investment option. Negative gearing should be seen as nothing more than a bonus to your investing plans, because it only applies to your relevant taxable income, and your personal circumstances are in a constant state of change. Like everyone else, investors change or lose jobs, their family dynamics alter, they retire, they invest in different types of trusts that incur different tax deductions, and so on – and all these factors have an impact on their depreciation options.

Stick with the fundamentals of smart investing and leave negative gearing to your accountant. And if anyone suggests negative gearing as a sole strategy for wealth building, consider them a bad choice of investment adviser.

## Chapter Hacks

- Strong cash flow keeps you afloat as an investor – remember that you still need to be able to service your loans.
- Cash-flow investing is useful as part of a diversified strategy, and there are some great ways to boost cash-flow returns.
- Capital growth is based on supply and demand.
- Look for capital growth drivers such as a diverse economic base, services, facilities and infrastructure.
- Compound growth is the secret sauce to capital growth.
- It's best to have a mix of cash-flow and capital growth properties in your portfolio.
- Never buy a property solely to benefit from negative gearing.

# 9

# Renovation

An entire genre of reality television has been devoted to the idea it takes little more than gumption, functioning limbs, basic management skills and a pop-up McCafe to guarantee a multi-million-dollar outcome through renovation.

Of course, anyone who has ever swung a hammer in the name of making a capital gain will tell you that renovation and construction upgrades are hard yakka – regardless of whether you're lifting the bricks or running the spreadsheet – and big results are not guaranteed.

Before you venture into this fascinating but fraught area of property investing, let's look at the different types of renovation.

Regardless of the eventual endgame for your renovation, there are generally two types of work you can undertake.

## Cosmetic renovation

Cosmetic work has been the go-to for the first-time DIYers for decades. 'Cosmetic work' isn't the name of the Kardashians' new television series, but rather it describes renovations you make below the existing roof line that do not involve altering the physical structure of the property.

It's seen by some as an easy way to riches: a lick of paint here, polish the floorboards there... wham, bam, thank you ma'am, money in the bank! Because you're not altering the basic layout of the home, you don't need to be concerned about the actual engineering of the structure. You've got what you've got, so you make the best of it.

As a kick-starter to the world of renovations, cosmetic work is great. Profitability, however, relies on keeping the buy-in price reasonable and ensuring the required touch-ups aren't too extensive.

## Cosmetic profits

As a rule of thumb, I think a cosmetic renovation should yield in the vicinity of 8 to 10 per cent on the money you tip in. So, if you're buying a house for $500,000 and putting $30,000 into the project, you effectively want to see a minimum end value of around $572,000.

## Structural renovation

At the other end of the scale is renovation work that requires the alteration of the structure of the property – you may be adding new rooms, knocking down external or internal walls or altering the roof line. Structural renovations can include removing a roof and building an additional storey, or even raising the main living area and creating more square metres underneath.

While it can appear daunting, undertaking structural renovations isn't necessarily that difficult. It does, however, require the assistance of your dream team – particularly building inspectors and structural engineers. If you're going to change the layout of a property, then load-bearing walls absolutely must be identified. Safety for both you and the end user is a non-negotiable, and specialist advice is essential in these circumstances.

Structural work might also see you altering the provision of services and utilities throughout the home, redirecting plumbing and electrical wiring in some circumstances. If this is the case, make sure you check in with a qualified tradesperson here as well.

Structural work tends to substantially increase the cost of renovation, so it's important to do a thorough due diligence (which I'll go through later in this chapter). Creating additional bedrooms or living spaces is all well and good, but if it costs $250,000 to build in a lower level and establish a fifth bedroom, you'd best make damn sure buyers or renters are looking for that sort of layout before you take on the heavy work.

## Structural profits

Because of the more complex and potentially risky nature of structural renovations, you should be expecting higher profits – in the vicinity of 12 to 15 per cent. These works are not for the faint-hearted. Typically, you'll need a lot more investment capital and longer timeframes.

You are probably going to have to tip $50,000 as a minimum into structural renovations – and from there the sky's the limit.

So, if you are buying a house for $500,000 and you are tipping in $50,000, you should essentially be looking for at least another 12 per cent on top of that $550,000 total. In this instance, I'd be very disappointed with a valuation that came in under $610,000 on completion. If my due diligence shows that this seems likely, I'll go back and see if I've made an error in my project planning, and even consider abandoning the project altogether.

## The golden rule of renovating

Regardless of your endgame, there's one iron-clad mantra you must make yours if you wish to come out ahead when you are doing renovation work: **this is a project for profit; it is not your home**.

The investor mindset dictates that you must not get caught up in the romance of creating a space you'd love to live in. While your imaginary dream home might include an internal water feature, trampoline room and studio for recording self-released hit songs, stepping beyond the basics is fraught with financial danger when you are renovating for sale or investment.

Think like an investor, not a homeowner.

## Why some renovations work... and some don't

The most crucial moment in any renovation project comes well before you start choosing hammer brands or paint shades. I'm talking about due diligence and the ability to remain unemotional and critical about the true costs and outcome for your project.

Don't be scared of deciding to not do a project. We all like to see a venture get underway, but you must be prepared to cut and run if the figures show a loss rather than a profit.

Let me talk you through my guidelines on doing a great job of the due diligence process.

### Know your endgame

There are two main options for what to do with a newly renovated property. You can either buy–renovate–sell (known as 'flipping') or buy–renovate–hold, with the latter meaning the finished project becomes part of your portfolio and will provide equity for further investment.

Both approaches rely on exactly the same result: they add maximum equity for minimum cost via smart upgrades.

Whether you then choose to release the equity by selling the asset and taking the cash or drawing down the equity and reinvesting is entirely up to you. In most cases, the numbers should be about the same. Think long and hard about your own personal strategy and portfolio and decide if the property fits in with your goals.

This common-sense approach will keep you on a straight path. Don't be tempted to change tack during the process unless there's a convincing reason – such as an unsolicited approach by a potential buyer willing to pay above the odds for your finished project.

Before you even take the plunge, run both scenarios on your renovation project. Do a comparison calculation of whether the hold or sell approach would achieve the best outcome for you in the long term. You need to be clear on your ideal endgame before you start.

If, as part of your strategy, you've located a suburb with excellent long-term growth and strong yields, rather than buying an impeccably finished home you may choose to take on a renovation. This will give you a lower buy-in price and the opportunity to create an investment that will appeal to local tenants and boost your balance sheet.

But remember our golden rule: this home is an investment. Do not renovate the property to your desired standard, but create a space that will maximise your rental yield so you can hold on for long-term capital growth.

If your property needs to appeal to shared house tenants such as students or groups of young professionals, try to create independent living spaces. Separate bathrooms are always going to be winners, and while the tenants might like to hang out with each other in the kitchen and on the deck, they'll need some 'alone time' in their private spaces too.

If the home is likely to appeal to a family, ensure your final room layout caters for that demographic. Are there multiple living spaces for families to do separate activities, as well as spaces where they can come together? Will it be pet friendly, if that's who you are appealing to? Are there adequate outdoor spaces to enjoy?

Knowing your likely tenant type will keep you on track so you don't make unnecessary decisions that can increase your costs without adding rental appeal.

If you plan to sell for profit, then your end user will again dictate the variables for your project.

An investor may want to buy your renovated home, but it's more likely a homeowner will be your target market when selling on. In this instance, you don't want to overspend – getting bang for your buck is the name of the game – but you may need to add a few extras that will ensure your offering stands out from the pack.

Try to work with the property's strengths. Enhance the available views, look at ways to create privacy, consider maximising available space and reducing unusable areas, and see what existing fittings and fixtures can be recycled and marketed as 'classic' inclusions.

Most importantly, take a look at what else is on offer in the neighbourhood and determine the price band in which you believe the finished venture will fit.

Renovating to sell can be a highly profitable option, but doing the numbers comprehensively, ahead of time, is an absolute must.

## Due diligence

Successful investors have due diligence so ingrained in their psyche that regardless of the investment type, most would roll their eyes at me suggesting it as an action point. However, while all real estate investments benefit from having a comprehensive due diligence process, renovation is one area in particular where any failure in proper analysis will almost certainly result in disaster.

Due diligence for renovation projects is a complex exercise too, because it involves you making decisions based on what you've determined the property's value to be both before and after the work, as well as on the estimated costs involved.

Let's go through the three main steps in the due diligence process. We need to start with working out the projected market value after renovation, then look into the overall project cost, and finally assess the market value before the renovation begins.

## Market value: after

Tackling the 'after' market value first seems counter-intuitive, but you'll soon see there's a method to my madness.

You'll need to have a good imagination and decent visualisation skills to assess the value of a property assuming all proposed works are completed.

First up, do a walk-through of the home. Assuming you've worked out the potential end user – whether buyer or renter – make note of what could be achievably changed that will improve its appeal in a cost-effective way. What will bring the home up to scratch? Put together a list of necessary works.

Here's a tip: walk through with your builder. They will be able to quickly tell you what work can be done and what might be challenging.

After you've built a picture in your mind of what the home will look like, apply the market approach. This is where you use other property sales to assess what the market will pay for your property once it is renovated. Ignore what it will cost to get your property there at this stage – just determine what its market worth would be.

Here's where you start to really work your mental muscles. You must come to understand your market through uncovering data of recent, local, similar sales. You can potentially look at sales as far back as six months, but don't be too retrospective. You want to read the market as it is 'now', not as it was 'then'.

Look for both recently sold renovated properties and those that are currently on the market. While actual completed sales are the most accurate source for assessing value, tracking current listings will help round out the picture – particularly in relation to buyer demand and potential competition for your finished project.

Try to find properties that are as similar as possible to what yours will be like once the works are completed. Are you renovating a colonial homestead on a 400 sqm site? Seek those comparable sales. Will yours be four-bedroom, two-bathroom when done? Again, looking at comparable sales for the same type of accommodation is a must.

Make sure the location is similar as well. Sales evidence within 500m of your prospect is best. This ensures you're comparing 'like with like' in relation to nearby services and facilities.

Finally, try to be dispassionate and analytical about the improvements you're comparing. It's hard not to feel to some degree that your renovation will be better than everybody else's – it's human nature – but it's to your advantage to keep a clear head with the analysis. If you feel you can't be dispassionate, ask a trusted property valuer or real estate agent (check in with your dream team!) to assist you.

Once you have the 'after' valuation in hand, it's time for the next step.

## Project cost

You now need to compile a reasonable estimate of what this deal will cost to complete:

- **Build cost** – first, lean on your trusted advisory builder to provide a broad but well-reasoned estimate of work. If it's a smaller, cosmetic renovation, you might be able to handle this step yourself. Make sure you include all elements of materials and labour, from paint and brushes to services such as plumbing and carpentry.

- **Professional fees** – you pay these fees to people such as engineers, designers and certifiers. This is one area of due diligence that people notoriously miss. Professional fees can run into thousands of dollars, so make sure you don't skimp when estimating these costs.
- **Fees and charges** – council rates, planning fees and charges are highly likely for structural renovation work. Set aside funds to account for these costs.
- **Contingency** – across all of the project costs, I like to allow a 10 per cent additional amount so there's a margin for error. If you don't use this contingency, great. If it's needed, you will be thankful it's there.
- **Buy-in and sell-out costs** – if the plan is to 'flip' the property, you'll be paying an agent to market and sell the finished home, and they'll earn a commission. There will also be costs associated with conveyancing. If you plan to retain the home in your portfolio, these sell-out costs can be removed, but you might need to allow for some lease-up costs.
- **Interest** – money doesn't come for free. If you are borrowing to complete the deal, don't forget to allow for interest on the spreadsheet too.
- **Profit** – why go through the exercise for free? As discussed, you must allow a margin of profit or equity gain in your calculations to reflect the riskiness of the venture. Working out what's 'reasonable' in this instance requires a little bit of experience. I've given you my thoughts on this. I would also encourage you to rely on your trusted team of advisers – particularly your property investment experts, your valuer or buyer's agent.

## Market value: before

This is where you decide what to pay for the property, and it involves using the data in two ways.

**The sales approach** is similar to the market approach you used to decide on the after-renovation figure. In this instance, however, unrenovated comparable sales are your friend.

When doing a before-renovation assessment of your potential purchase, I believe looking at house sales with similar land size (or floor area for a unit) is imperative. This will keep your comparison consistent. Attempting to compare your prospective property with substantially larger or smaller allotments will skew your ability to compare effectively.

When weighing up your dwelling against others, you must be brutal in your opinion. Compared to the sales evidence, does your potential project need substantially more work to bring it up to scratch? Don't lie to yourself – these are real dollars you're playing with here. If you psychologically 'gloss over' the amount of work to be done, you will only hurt yourself in the long run. Again, an agent or valuer will prove helpful if you're having trouble.

The second approach to the 'before' assessment of value, **the cost approach**, requires some other numbers that you've already gathered.

Put simply, take your after-renovation valuation, deduct all the project costs and see where you end up. You've done the hard work to make this assessment as accurate as possible. The resulting figure is the maximum you should pay for the property based on the information you have available right now.

Now compare the two pre-renovation assessments you've just done. Do they look about the same? This is the time to check and recheck your calculations, because your assessment of these numbers will determine if you're in with a chance of scoring a very handy deal.

If your cost approach figure is greater than your sales approach figure, you have found a hot prospect. It means that you have the ability to pay a little more than market value (not that you will, of course!) and still turn a profit.

On the flipside, if the cost approach has you paying more than the market approach, then you need to either abandon the project and look for a better investment or find a way to reduce the project costs.

## Opportunity cost

Don't discount opportunity cost in your due diligence. Of the various types of residential real estate investment, renovation projects will take up more of your 'spare' time over a short period, so allowing for opportunity cost is essential.

Opportunity cost recognises that by investing time, money or effort into a project, you are not devoting those resources to another deal and thus missing out on potential gains from that alternative deal.

Say you decide on a structural renovation project and due diligence shows that after six months of purchasing, planning and execution, you'd sell for a clean profit of $40,000. That sounds pretty handy.

Also imagine that you are a corporate lawyer earning $300,000 net per year. To complete this project, you'd need to take eight weeks off work and wield a paintbrush, swing a hammer, backfill a garden bed and do the project management.

Those four weeks would cost you around $45,000 in lost income. You wouldn't want to do the job for only $5,000 profit – it's too risky.

Always remember to consider what would be the best use of your time. Make sure the figures stack up.

## Avoid overcapitalisation

Now it's time to talk about something that should be avoided at all cost (excuse the pun) – the big 'O' of overcapitalisation.

Overcapitalisation occurs when you spend more money on a renovation or improvement than it's likely to yield in added value. If you spend $200,000 on an improvement but it only adds $100,000 in value, that's overcapitalisation.

The risk of overcapitalisation is the bane of every renovator's existence. It's hard to manage because often emotions get in the way.

It exists because people repeatedly ignore the simple truism that cost does not equal value. Buyers don't surmise that because you spent $100,000 renovating a $500,000 home, they should pay $600,000 for it. Buyers can choose from multiple homes in an area and weigh up the pros and cons of each before deciding on the price they want to pay. To be brutal, they don't care what it cost you, they just want to pay as little as possible for what they want among a selection of properties.

Pools are an excellent example of how to overcapitalise. Say you grew up on the sunny North Shore of Sydney in an upwardly mobile suburb. You loved having a pool. Neighbours and friends came over and built some of their grandest memories around your 'cement pond'. It was a way to relax and enjoy your family home.

Now, let's imagine you're tackling your first renovation project in one of the more affordable locations in southeast Queensland. You may think, *I had a pool – it was great! Surely the new owners of my project would like one too?*

Well, here's a little tip I learned long ago. When you're planning to renovate, look over fences. Except in specific circumstances (such as at the extreme upper price sector of the market), you should avoid adding anything to the home that isn't already well accepted and established in neighbouring properties.

If your neighbours don't have pools, think twice, because it means buyers are unlikely to pay what the pool costs to put in. I chose this example because valuers have told me a pool that costs $50,000 to install might add as little as $25,000 to the market value in the wrong suburb.

Here's what valuers ask themselves when identifying over-capitalisation of a pool: 'If there are two homes side by side, identical in every way except one has a pool and the other doesn't, based on my comparable sales evidence, how much more would a reasonable buyer pay for the one with the pool regardless of what it cost?'

With a bit of experience, you can apply this thinking to all sorts of items in a house – from kitchen fit-out to deck finishes to floor and wall coverings. For each item, ask yourself if your end buyer would pay as much as it would cost you to install.

## The false-positive result

In the renovation industry, everyone loves a success story. It's one where there are plenty of photos and a smiling couple sitting on the porch of their stunning project, proclaiming that they made a profit for minimal outlay. It all looks too easy… but there's one great big elephant in the room being conveniently left out when these tales are told.

It's the property market 'false positive', where capital gains are attributed to the renovation when they simply resulted from market values rising more generally.

For those of us in the property advisory profession, it's incredibly frustrating. This is why due diligence must include an assessment of the end value before you jump into a venture.

It's just been far too common – particularly in the periods from 2012 to 2017 and 2019 to 2022 in Sydney. This harbour city is filled with examples of 'masterminds' who bought a house for $1.5 million, did a renovation, sold for $2.5 million and pro-claimed their genius to the world.

If they bothered to break it down correctly, yes, they sold for $2.5 million, but from that, they paid $1.5 million for the home, $65,500 in stamp duty, they did a $400,000 renovation, and in the three years they held the property and lived in it and didn't pay CGT, the market moved 55 per cent!

If I deducted $25,000 in cash deposit, and $65,500 in stamp duty and other holding costs, would I have achieved the same outcome? Could I have bought another property in that same market with that same growth? Absolutely! I could walk backwards through those calculations and inform these renovation prodigies, 'Guys, if you didn't do that project and instead just bought another property in the last five years and held onto it, you would have made $550,000 without doing anything'.

With renovation due diligence, it pays to be smart, not busy. Don't take credit for a strengthening market. In the Sydney example, they just got lucky.

## My top three tips for renovators

To round out the discussion on renovation as an investment option, I want to leave you with three important guidelines. By adopting these habits you'll avoid a heap of heartache.

### 1. Keep impeccable records of costs

Renovation projects require a keen eye for detail and the ability to stay on top of costs and timelines, because the financial bene-fits and penalties flow from your ability to watch both the dollars and minutes.

Make sure you track every cent going out the door. Money spent on the pest inspection during the settlement phase, what you paid for handles for the new cabinets, interest payments to the bank and the advertising spend when it came time to sell – every cent is important.

Why? Well, first, every bit of money you hand to someone else for goods or services is coming straight off your bottom line. Tracking costs will help you stay on top of the cash flow and translate into the frugal habits that will maximise your return on every single dollar.

Second, tracking expenses provides a lesson in costing projects that will be etched into your memory bank. When you move onto the next project and an electrician tries to stitch you up with an over-the-top quote, you'll be onto him.

Finally, these figures will all be deductible in some fashion come tax time. Avoid the stress when June 30 approaches. Instead, document progressively so your accountant knows exactly how the project played out.

My other tip about costs is to get a depreciation schedule ASAP if you are retaining the property in your portfolio. Depreciation schedules allow you to offset a percentage of the cost of a fitting or fixture as a progressive 'wear and tear' amount. Talk to a specialist quantity surveyor about putting together a schedule. The cost of the report is often recouped in the first year. Best of all, you only need one report for the entire lifecycle of the property investment, so it's a cost-effective activity.

## 2. Take a lot of before and after photos

I bloody love property, so you won't be surprised to hear that I am snap happy with my renovations and builds.

I suggest you adopt the same approach. Comprehensive photos before, during and after the project are more than simply a keepsake. If you are looking to sell the property, these snaps can form part of an effective marketing campaign. I know of journalists who have profiled renovations for their newspapers simply because the before and after photos of the renovation were so dramatic.

The other reason for having lots of photos is even more practical. If you are looking to retain the property, you will be visiting your financier for a revaluation. Supplying photos (along with your comprehensive documentation of costs) can help your case when arguing for an increase in value. While a valuer will base their assessment on comparable sales and what they see during the inspection, your photos can help paint the picture. Valuers will take note of what you paid for the property, which in this case is pre-renovation. Happy snaps prove you have put a heap of work into the project to elevate the equity.

### 3. Do what you can, but outsource the rest

Most of us can wield a paintbrush and dig a hole, but there are times when you should sit back and leave it to the experts.

The first instance is for those obvious tasks that you are wholly unqualified to do, such as electrical and plumbing work. Otherwise the outcome is bound to be a disaster, whether it's work that will need to be ripped out and replaced or, worse, a hospital visit.

Know your skill limits and seek assistance. If you do want to try tiling or wallpaper hanging, at the very least do a short course and see how you get on. DIY can be satisfying, but stay safe and smart.

The second reason to outsource comes back to the opportunity cost. One of my clients, who is also a mate, talks about the time they did a small renovation prior to the birth of their first child. This professional couple weren't new to doing some handiwork, so the idea of painting the baby's room didn't seem too daunting.

So they went ahead. Every weekend and most spare evenings for three weeks, they sanded the walls, filled the gaps and prepared the surface. They taped up windows and light fixtures, moved furniture and placed drop sheets throughout. Then they painted: undercoat, first coat and second coat.

Their miscalculation? The couple were both highly paid professionals whose hourly rate was very impressive. They also had precious little spare time – so, for close to a month, every minute seemed to be spent in that room. It became more a prison than a project.

Once done, my mate admitted it was the worst paint job he'd ever seen – and he was a property professional.

The kicker? This same couple had their whole house painted a year later, when they decided to move out but retain the home as an investment. Their contractors completed the job in five days. It looked excellent for the tenants. On top of that, the painters did the job for half of what this pair would have earned instead of doing the baby's room.

They could have worked the equivalent hours, paid painters and still been well ahead in their bank balance.

Know your worth and how best to spend your precious time – or live in regret and have a tale of sorrow to tell your mates. It's your choice.

## Chapter Hacks

- Always run the numbers first when deciding on either cosmetic or structural renovation work, then track expenses as you go along.
- A structural renovation should ideally return a 12 to 15 per cent profit on the buy-in cost plus project cost.

- Remember the golden rule of renovating: this is a project for profit; it is not your home.
- Work out your endgame before you start: either renovating to sell or hold.
- Following a comprehensive due diligence process – including working out opportunity cost – is essential.
- Avoid overcapitalisation.

# 10

# House and land

Succeeding at something new is satisfying. Most times, it's some small, incremental gain in knowledge and skill that builds on your experience and propels you ever closer to expert level. When you come out the other side of a new challenge, take a moment to stand back with a smile on your face and think, *Look what I just did... not too bad!*

Property is full of seemingly small victories that snowball so you can proudly wear the 'experienced investor' badge. I believe one of the most gratifying tick-box moments that always adds a new dimension to the journey is a first house and land (H&L) project.

The construction of a new house on a selected block has become easier over recent years. Advances in building materials and techniques mean specialist contractors can often achieve their clients' brief in record time, which in turn helps owners get in tenants sooner to crank up the cash flow or be able to sell for profit.

However, it's not the sort of venture you should blunder into without a little insider knowledge. There are a few tips and tricks for the first-timer that need to be taken into account.

## What is house and land?

An H&L project refers to an endeavour to construct an entirely new home on a vacant standard-size residential allotment.

These projects most often occur in new residential estates located in a region's population growth zone. You might even begin the process of an H&L deal before the block has been created, as part of a comprehensive multi-stage development.

That said, you can of course construct an investment house on any available site. Given increasing population densities in major capital cities, H&L projects can crop up wherever a new piece of dirt has been reclaimed.

We'll tackle small development later in this chapter, but imaginative splitter block and small subdivision work seems capable of unearthing liveable spaces in major cities where it seems no more could fit.

H&L projects can be highly lucrative if you have the right guidance through the process, but you must weigh up the costs and benefits.

## The upside of H&L

Starting with a clean slate offers some great advantages for investors. First and foremost, you aren't tethered to a home's pre-existing design. Depending on your desired outcome, you can tailor the construction to maximise the return on investment you're shooting for.

Here's an example. Let's say you pick a growth corridor in the western suburbs of a major capital which is seeing progressive value gains in house prices and strong tenant demand.

A multi-stage residential project is catering to the educational, service and convenience needs of its local populace. A train line extension has improved the work commute for a huge number of residents, and a hot run of property prices in the inner city has pushed modest-income households out toward this new community.

You may choose to build and retain your property and cater for a family tenant. The average renter demographic is a couple with two kids. One of the parents travels to work each day and the other is likely to be working part time from home.

After selecting and locating an appropriately priced allotment, you can design and construct a holding that will appeal to that demographic. In this case that includes a minimum of four bedrooms (or three bedrooms with a functional and practical home office for remote working), an informal, open plan design with useable living spaces and a double lock-up garage. Tenants here demand air-conditioning, security screens and covered outdoor living but need low-maintenance gardens.

While you might search through the local listings, the chance of the perfect property being up for sale is slim. The fact is, you have an opportunity to create it through an H&L deal, allowing you to maximise the rent, minimise the vacancy and hold for longer to let capital gains kick in.

Another advantage is that new builds invariably come with greater depreciation allowances than existing homes. A qualified quantity surveyor will be able to prepare a report for you on your new construction, which would identify those fittings and fixtures with a 'depreciable value'. While I won't get into the complexities of legislation and depreciation cost calculations, it's fair to say that new homes carry a substantial allowance that can dramatically reduce your taxable income each year. While investing in property purely for tax advantages is absolutely not advisable, the sweetener of the new-home depreciation schedule is very handy for investors.

A further upside for younger investors is potential government assistance. Depending on how they tackle the build and how it will fit into their portfolio, young first-time investors might consider it feasible to build a property as a first home in order to take advantage of concessions and rebates offered by their state government. At an appropriate time, this home could be converted into an investment to start a portfolio.

## The downside to H&L

As an investment option, there are counter-considerations to all those advantages too.

First, new homes do seem to carry a 'new car' premium with them. By this, I mean the cost of H&L can often be greater than buying a similar property in the same location that is a year or two older. There are strategies to mitigate this premium through builder selection and negotiation, but an analysis of multiple similar homes comparing 'new' with 'used' will generally show the newest builds costing most. This issue is particularly relevant in the market today. From 2021 to 2023, there were substantial increases in the cost of construction – and many experts believe they will continue for some time yet. Be certain you do all you can to reduce these costs without compromising too much on the fundamentals that make for a good investment asset in your location of interest.

The other obvious downside is that new construction in residential estates can be a bit vanilla, with similar home styles and finishes. Economics 101 says if supply is high at a certain level of demand, potential price growth is more subdued. If a buyer or tenant is spoiled for choice because there are plenty of similar options available, then it will be harder to get a substantial premium on resale in the short term, or a boosted rental.

## How to win with H&L

On balance, a great H&L deal might be perfect for your portfolio at a particular stage of your investment journey, but what are the keys to striking a winning outcome?

### Know your goal

It's becoming a theme in this book, isn't it?

Before a single contract is signed you must be fully aware of your endgame. It's no good sinking hundreds of thousands of dollars into a dwelling design that caters for tenants if your intention is to sell to an owner-occupier on completion. It's nonsensical to put in high-maintenance improvements such as a pool or detailed gardens when you're hoping to appeal to a family tenant.

Know your end user well. Once you've decided whether you want to sell or retain the investment, dig into the demographics. Talk to local agents and property managers. Work out how to maximise your sale price or rent through ensuring your property caters to the needs of its eventual resident.

### Select land wisely

As in all things real estate, location drives smart decisions.

When selecting your vacant block, whether in a new estate or an established suburb, ensure it includes all the fundamentals that will attract your end user.

Quiet, elevated sites with easy access (walkable if possible) to convenience facilities and lifestyle hubs will always appeal.

The physical attributes of a site are extra important when you're building a new property. Flat blocks are substantially cheaper to build on than sloping sites. Stable soil types will reduce the cost of foundations, as will avoiding building in areas known for sub-surface boulders.

You also need adequate site dimensions so your frontage allows for easy access. And your home's setback from the boundary is going to have an impact on your design.

The site is where you start with H&L – get it right, right from the get-go.

## Get multiple quotes

For first-timers in this space, building contracts will be an enigma, wrapped in a mystery and tied with a question mark. They are an interesting mix of legal details, construction checklists, spurious variation allowances and steadfast schedules. Even the smartest of buyers can be baffled, because this is a world they rarely venture into.

My first suggestion is to make sure everything you want in your build is covered under the contract. I will go into the level of detail my wife and I employ in our builds later. Suffice it to say, we know exactly what our specifications are – down to the number of power points – before we even begin to seek builders' quotes.

Also, obtain three quotes. This is one area in which simply asking for comparable quotes could end up saving you tens of thousands of dollars. Make sure you're comparing like with like in terms of inclusions, and don't necessarily go for the cheapest quote.

If in doubt, your independent designer or architect and quantity surveyor can help cut through the jargon and reveal the time, cost and quality details of each contract.

## Lean on your dream team

Now is not the time to try a barrel ride in the hollow of a wave (that's an advanced surfing manoeuvre, by the way).

Your dream team are there to help save you. I have heard hundreds of stories of builds going bad because an owner made assumptions about a deal that resulted in a bad decision.

For example, I'm aware of a gent who built a home under a standard contract with a project-style builder. It had a good sized floor area, reasonably priced. After holes had been cut in the plasterboard for recessed lights, he noticed there was only one light fitting in each room, including the living room. He asked the builder for a variation to make it four fittings per room.

'Sure,' said the builder. 'Under the contract the variation is $400 per fitting – so that's $1,600 per room by eight rooms – that'll be $12,800.'

Your solicitor and designer will be able to help you with the contract details. Your buyer's agent can assist with land selection, and your accountant can help with ownership structures and tax issues.

You may also want to think about employing your own project manager for the build. This professional will know their way around house plans, will be your eyes and ears onsite and can deal with any sticky issues. They can make decisions that are in your best interests and instruct the builder and subcontractors on what you require.

Don't tackle the challenge alone. Rely on good advice.

Taking on an H&L project is exciting. Fast-forwarding to the project's completion, standing in your completed holding with keys in hand should give you a sense of accomplishment and satisfaction, not anxiety.

## Development

Spend a little time with a group of your favourite investment buddies and you'll no doubt come across those souls who've tackled a small development project.

These gatherings can be a little like a group of mates getting together after a satisfying surf session to swap tales about extraordinary waves. Most will be keen to retell the story of a particularly fine line they adopted down the face with a convincing bottom turn that took them back up the lip before executing a floating re-entry that would have made Kelly Slater proud.

Sweet!

But there are other stories, perhaps told less frequently... about a poorly timed paddle that saw the surfer tumble over the falls and kiss the reef. Or a misstep that produced an ungraceful exit as their weight shifted one way while the board went the other. Or maybe it was an embarrassing call of 'Mine!' that had all others on the outside exit... only to watch them flail, then fail, and pull off the wave.

In the same way, small developers will happily recount tales about projects where clever strategy helped them yield impressive results – but for every winning decision, there's another less profitable outcome where the downfall was fuelled by inexperience or lack of caution.

I recently took on a client who sold her house in Caringbah on a six-month settlement – an old fibro shack on 600-plus sqm – to a first-time developer for $1,550,000.

The purchaser was keen – too keen, it seems. No sooner had they taken possession than they ploughed down the old structure in preparation for building. The thing is, this buyer hadn't received approval for their proposed project. They were locked up for ages in planning, paying approximately $15,000 per month in interest while watching the market soften.

I know what high-end duplexes cost to build in this local authority, as I've completed a number of them myself. That purchaser would have needed to spend $1.3 million at the time to produce the sort of product that would work in this market. In the end, they made a loss of close to $100,000 because they failed to do comprehensive due diligence and proceeded without thought.

As a property strategy, small developments could fill several volumes with encyclopaedic detail. We'll cover much of what you'll need to know here, but it really is just dipping your toes in the development surf. Experience can be a tough tutor when it comes to small development, so proceed warily. Small development can offer impressive upsides, but great profit often comes with an equal share of risk.

## Small development types

Let's take a look at this small development space and see what options are available to the active investor.

At one end of the spectrum is land subdivision, which is generally considered the simplest, lowest-risk way to get your feet wet in the small development space. At the other end of the spectrum are construction projects, which carry higher risk and reward. In between is a raft of options that will help build your confidence and skills.

Here's a summary of small development projects, from easiest to most challenging:

- **Block splits** is when a site is held under a single title but is already described by two or more lots. Under this arrangement, an investor may choose to go through a process of retitling that will result in separate titles being issued for each lot or block. While generally considered the lowest risk of all small projects, they're difficult to locate and yield a relatively small profit margin.

- **Subdivision** is when a large site is resurveyed and subdivided into two or more new blocks. Subdivision requires a little more effort, with application and approval all part of the deal. This is a slightly higher-risk type of project than retitling but still eagerly sought after by low-risk, low-margin small developers.

- **Split and shift** is a general term that describes subdividing a block on which an existing house is being retained. In these projects, the home will often be centrally located on the block. As such, when the block is split or subdivided, the dwelling will need to be moved onto one of the newly created sites – hence the block is 'split' and the home is 'shifted'.

- **Strata titling** is a technique predominately used to create separate titles on an existing property where multiple dwelling units already exist. The most obvious example of this process is the strata titling of existing flats, where a block of flats sitting on a single title is resurveyed onto a plan with separate titles issued. These projects can yield impressive profits, but they are increasingly rare. Single-title multiple residential properties were a hallmark of Australia last century. Since the advent of group titles, building unit plans and survey plans, most new construction will already hold the block in separate titles – even if the developer intends to retain the lot for its rental income. We may see this revert a little given the potential for built-to-rent projects to gain a foothold, but all in all, single-title multi-living structures are rare nowadays.

- **Additional dwellings** is a general term that describes the construction of additional accommodation on a property that has an existing home. For some, it's the granny flat (or ancillary dwelling, as discussed in Chapter 8), which might allow you to generate extra income and boost yield. Another variation is where zoning, site dimension, land area and existing home placement might allow for the construction of townhouses in a backyard. Small construction projects like these do embody slightly more risk and potential reward, and as such they're not recommended for novices who've never previously attempted a development of any sort.

- **New build strata (townhouses and apartments)** is where we begin to head toward more complex projects, such as six-pack, three-storey walk-up units or small townhouse complexes, needing a wide range of skills from project management and town planning through to financial awareness and market analysis (think dream team). Returns within this space can be outstanding, as long as you have the proper support of the skills and specialisations of your dream team. You only need flip through the *Australian Financial Review (AFR) Rich List* each year to spot the number of millionaires and billionaires who've made serious coin through property development. But with great reward comes great risk, and it would be foolish to jump into this style of investment without learning to surf the smaller-wave deals first. Some low-risk ways to gain experience in construction include via mentors and JV partners.

- **Mix 'n' match** projects have a number of different elements. For example, a split and shift might also require a renovation and the construction of an ancillary dwelling. You might also do a split and shift to create space for the construction of a couple of townhouses in the newly increased backyard. Just remember – increasing the complexity of the project means you're increasing the risk and, by rights, should mean you also increase the potential profit.

## The development cycle

The stages of the development cycle are generally consistent, regardless of what style of development project you're looking to tackle.

## The acquisition stage

The acquisition stage is not as simple as spotting an advertised development site in your local listing pages, signing on the dotted line and sitting back waiting for the profit to come in.

Acquiring a development site is a highly detailed process that requires vigilance and resourcefulness. In addition, while you may desire enough time to carefully consider which deals have the best potential, you'll also need to be quick on your feet when you come across a profitable venture. Profitable development sites are highly prized among the pool of canny buyers – you snooze, you lose.

The first step is **sourcing sites**. Here's where you need a little hustle, because sourcing development sites requires what my grandparents would have called 'a bit of gumption'.

While you can try looking through listings on property portals, this method will rarely present a golden opportunity to the casual developer. At the very least, you must set up list alerts on sites like realestate.com.au or domain.com.au so you will be notified whenever a property that fits your predefined criteria is listed for sale.

Begin with locations that offer opportunities within your price range and risk tolerance. Set up several alerts for locations in which you know your proposed 'end product' will be appealing.

There's a general rule in the property development sphere, however – if a site has hit the portals, three other potential buyers have already rejected it. So, how do you become the first to see a potential site and not the last?

Next, **draw on your networks**. Build rapport with local agents, your dream team and their professional associates, and any other useful investment community members you can think of. Let everyone know that you're on the hunt for a deal. Make sure they're aware of what type of venture you want.

Next is **cold calling**. This is exactly what I do in my buyer's agent role every day. It can be exhausting and time consuming, but push on, because only tenacity brings results in this game.

There's also the option of cold calling for sites. Don't baulk at this – some of the best deals I know have happened because somebody made the effort to reach out and see if an owner was willing to sell.

One of my associates a few years back was doing the rounds of Saturday morning inspections when he discovered an excellent block of land with a postwar home. The thing was, it wasn't on the market. He could see the split potential and thought, *What the hell, I'll give it a shot.* After drafting a handwritten note and dropping it in the mailbox, he was excited to receive a phone call just a few days later from the owner's son. As it turned out, his elderly mum had recently passed away and he and his siblings were in the process of settling her assets, including this rental property – would my mate be up for a chat?

Without the intervention of an agent, they reached an agreement which saw a smooth transition of the property for a reasonable price. The family sellers were happy with the quick, painless transfer of the property and the small developer buyer made a tidy profit. And it was all because of politely worded correspondence.

There are few shortcuts to the sourcing phase, but with patience, skill and effort, you will uncover a potential project.

At this preliminary stage, you will want to conduct a quick **initial analysis** of a project's potential, primarily to weed out those that are not worth going ahead with.

During my property education years, I loved reading small developer profiles in national property magazines. I came across one about a developer who had completed many profitable projects in southeast Queensland. His success was built on generous buffer allowances and conservative costs, plus most of his deals were quick turnarounds with profits exceeding $100,000 each.

How did he do it? By sheer weight of numbers and fast analysis.

This young bloke said he would easily consider over 100 potential projects before coming across 10 that might fit his criteria. From those 10, a deeper dive would reveal the handful of options worth further investigation.

His approach was to become the expert in his markets of interest. He set himself an ambitious goal: to be able to conduct a preliminary due diligence within one hour of finding a site which would tell him whether to continue following the wave or head back to the beach.

That's right – one hour. As a small developer, you must become adept at conducting back-of-the-napkin analysis, because an agent or owner will often need a quick 'Yes' or 'No' so they can decide whether to stick with you or move on to the next potential buyer.

To do this properly, you must also be across what you'll likely sell the end product for, how much it will cost to get there and what you can afford to pay for the site so you retain an acceptable profit. All of this comes with experience and relying on your trusted advisers.

Don't waste time on unprofitable deals. Move fast, think quickly and be ruthless.

So, you're happy with numbers and keen to strike a deal. It's time to start looking at **negotiation** and how to secure a contract.

While price will always be a factor – it's said that you make your money when you buy, not when you sell – development site acquisition offers some unique opportunities for building immediate profitability through thoughtful contract clauses.

The foundation of this is that time equals money, because the longer you're carrying your borrowed funds, the more interest you'll have to outlay.

With this in mind, consider the following options when looking to snap up a development site (it goes without saying that your solicitor must be across any contract for purchasing a small project site):

- **Delayed settlement.** This is not about adding time for the sake of it. Asking for longer settlement allows you to plan how you'll effectively space out costs and tasks, conduct your due diligence (see more about this later in this chapter) and shop around for the best quotes without having to fork out the entire purchase price too quickly. Delaying settlement will also enable you to plot out your project timeline so you have the most efficient process once it begins. For example, you may need to bring in a preferred builder for demolition and construction, but he is tied up on a project for the next three months. Delaying settlement allows you to keep the huge holding cost of interest at bay while waiting for the builder to be available. This time buffer also provides the opportunity to line up the first task ready to get stuck into, with all others following in an orderly fashion – quickly, efficiently and, ultimately, more profitably.

- **Early access.** As you may have gathered, efficiencies are key when it comes to small projects. Having an early access clause allows you and your contractors to carry out some nonintrusive works that will speed up the project once you take possession. For example, subdivision will require site assessments and surveys as part of the approval process. Early access is where the seller allows you and your contractors to come onsite for the purposes of conducting due diligence or preparing quotes. In some circumstances, early access might enable some minor preparations to be done for demolition works, or activity such as a surveyor pegging the property. Most reasonable vendors will allow early access, so make sure it's included in the deal.

- **Subject to due diligence / subject to approval.** These are great clauses to include as part of the deal because they mitigate risks. Buying subject to due diligence allows you to secure the property before you've completed all your research. A subject to due diligence clause builds in a defined period – say, seven days – in which you can conduct more thorough research into the project's viability. If during that time you discover the deal is a dud, you can pull out of the contract with little to no penalty. A subject to approval clause allows you, as the purchaser, to start the development approval process before settlement has been completed. If the local authority denies your plans or places overly difficult development conditions on the proposal, you can again pull out of the purchase at little to no penalty. 'Subject to' clauses need to be used in conjunction with 'early access' clauses, of course. You also need to bear in mind the project's anticipated sale price when considering which clauses to request for inclusion in the contract.

## The due diligence stage

I cannot stress enough how imperative it is to conduct due diligence work as part of a project. Due diligence is where you must back up your opinions with facts and be prepared to walk away if the numbers fail to stack up. We've discussed the due diligence process for renovation work (see Chapter 9) and here we focus on it in relation to developments.

There are three primary questions to ask during due diligence of a small development project.

### 1. What will I sell my end product for? (Gross realisation)

Whether it's a vacant block of land, a relocated house or newly constructed units and townhouses, your end product sale price assessment must be based on recent comparable sales evidence.

Getting this figure right is so important that I urge you to have an independent professional do an audit of your findings and ask hard questions. It's very easy for novice investors to get caught up in their own projects and apply a special premium to their intended stock. 'My townhouses will be heaps better than everyone else's in this area, so I'll get much better prices,' is a common example of the rose-coloured approach some grommet developers apply. However, overestimating your end figure has dire consequences down the line.

My next tip is to err on the side of caution. Try to settle on the conservative end of your value estimate ranges. You don't want any nasty surprises where you fail to reach expectations come the end of the process.

### 2. What will it cost to complete the project?

This question really needs to be answered in consultation with your dream team.

Development costs aren't just for the obvious outlays on things like house demolition or construction work. Development costs need to be all-encompassing.

Here is my checklist of all costs:

- Civil construction/physical development costs
- Professional fees – e.g. surveyor, town planner, project manager

- Council fees and charges – e.g. rates, headworks costs, application fees
- Buy-in and sell-out costs including marketing and commissions
- Interest charges – on both development costs and property purchase
- Contingency – a buffer allowance of an additional 10 per cent on all costs to cover any unforeseen shortfall.

### 3. How much profit is there and over what timeframe is it earned?

You need to get paid for your efforts – no one should be doing this for free!

Your acceptable return on investment will depend on the project's risk and the time needed to complete the venture. For example, if you're doing a simple block split that will take three months to complete, you might feel a $50,000 profit is pretty impressive. But if you're tackling a split and shift where you'll also create two new townhouses in the backyard, and that process will involve 12 months of approvals and labour, $50,000 will be nowhere near enough.

Determining adequate profit to properly balance risk and opportunity cost against the potential reward takes a bit of experience. I'd suggest you lean on your professional advisers and mentors so you can determine what the minimum acceptable return will be for you.

By answering these three due diligence questions, you can now deduct the total costs and desired profit from the end sale price or gross realisation figure. The residual amount will give you a round figure of what you can afford to pay for the property. If this figure falls at or under the asking price, you could be onto a winner.

## The development and construction stage

The development stage realistically begins the moment you engage your town planner to begin the process of assessing the options and gaining acceptable development approvals.

A good town planner will take on the role of your guide and mentor by helping you maximise the possibilities. In conjunction with surveyors and designers, they will look at what is permissible and arguable under a town plan so you yield the best possible result.

It's at this stage that town planners and designers really come into their own. Experienced planners will often gain a little extra floor space or slightly more relaxed boundary setbacks. In some cases, they may even be able to successfully argue a proposal that seems to fall outside the town plan. Listen to them and draw on their guidance.

Construction is the epic moment for many small developers. It's that real-deal stage when they see the machinery do its thing while the site is crawling with tradies and their apprentices. It's both exciting and confronting.

Construction management is not beyond the scope of most sensible humans when it comes to small projects like block splits. By following the lead of your town planner, surveyor and solicitor, you should be able to navigate the path to approval and completion.

When it comes to managing multiple suppliers and labourers on a more complex deal, however, consider how much you want to outsource to others. This stage is very much about managing timing, cost and quality – the three hallmarks of every project. If you feel this would take you out of your depth, seek help. There are always dream team members, mentors and JV partners who can assist you.

For many, using a professional project manager will be the go. These people work for you, fighting the necessary battles and making the best decisions in order to bring in your project within expectations.

Overall, you have to consider whether you are comfortable being uncomfortable, because the stresses of managing a development project can be immense. Having the right mindset will help too, of course. Becoming mentally prepared to tackle the stresses is as important as any other element of small development.

Here are four tips on how best to manage the development and construction phase.

As mentioned in the section on negotiating contracts, **early access** to the site – even prior to settlement – is extremely handy for co-ordinating construction quotes and completing nonintrusive early work. However, don't proceed with anything substantial until you own the property. I have heard real-life horror stories about small developers paying for approvals and beginning works prior to settlement only to have the contract fall over on a technicality.

It's common sense but worth repeating: **get multiple quotes**. Ensure you aren't just saying yes to the first quote put in front of you for any major works.

While reputable businesses will hopefully always provide reasonable estimates, an under-the-pump contractor may include an extraordinarily high margin in their quote. Crosscheck that what you're getting in the quote is right, and even seek the advice of a quantity surveyor. They're an excellent safety net for first-time developers.

**Study the details.** One of the hidden traps for amateurs choosing a fixed-price building contract is a failure to understand exactly what they're getting for their money. When you're comparing quotes, you must be able to compare like with like.

For example, builders like to apply a provisional cost (PC) amount in contracts. They might say, 'We'll allow $20,000 for bathroom fit-out but won't specify exactly what items are included in the contract'. This sounds great, except those who don't study the details might discover that to achieve the end result they want, the cost of fitting out the bathrooms is actually $30,000 apiece.

Check if the product you think you're going to get is the product you're actually going to get. Is there a list of additional PC items that you need to go through? Are you able to compare builders, knowing exactly what each is including?

On a development we did, my wife and I were so detailed in our research that we had folders too full of documents to be closed properly. They were chock-a-block with plans and specifications built up over several months. We'd been working closely with our JV partner and architect to understand each nuance and took in so much information I could walk through the finished town-houses in my head before a sod of earth had even been turned.

This approach was invaluable when it came time to select the builder. We were immediately on the front foot and knew all the particulars better than the builder when it came time to lock in the construction contract.

**Be present and seek help.** As any surfer will know, if you hesitate on the take-off, you'll be pitched over the falls.

Make sure you, or a trusted representative, are keeping track of the building progress and are on hand to make decisions. A site left entirely to its own devices will fall behind schedule and over budget. Regular meetings with your head contractor to discuss issues are a must, while staying on top of the finances is imperative if you don't want to be left short of funds during the build.

I've seen just about as many developments fail through neglect as through bad decision-making or lousy luck. Remember – neglect can be fixed just by showing up.

## The completion stage

It's at or just prior to completion that the fun begins to ramp up a notch.

Early on in the due diligence stage, you started making some decisions on what you'd like to do with the project once completed. Would you like to hold onto the finished product as part of your portfolio, or look to sell and take the profit? You may decide to change this decision at completion because you'll want to reflect on the most current market conditions and your own personal position.

There is no right answer as to what to do – it's a very personal choice. The overriding consideration will be whether the completed product is an investment-worthy asset that will fit within your portfolio and perform as needed for your long-term strategic plan.

The choice to hold on and not sell does have benefits. Some of those include reduced taxation outcomes and depreciation upsides.

Selling also has its appeal. You get to release the profit and choose how to use the funds. Will you move on to your next project? Will you purchase an established growth asset? Or is it time to pay down some debt? Cash is freedom, and you are in control of your own destiny. My only caveat is to make sure your cash keeps working for you. Don't let it sit. If you can retain it in completed developed stock where it's doing its compounding magic rather than sitting in a bank account falling in value against inflation, then why sell down?

My final tip about completion is this: if you complete and decide to sell, seek the services of an agent with experience in the particular product you've developed. Look for a local who knows exactly what type of buyers will be keen for your end product. Not only will they be able to guide you on price and appropriate marketing, they might already have potential buyers on their books.

Small developments are a lucrative way for investors to build wealth, but they aren't for the first-timer. With planning, persistence and support, they can be a success, but don't bluster in underprepared and find yourself out of your depth.

## Chapter Hacks

- The advantages of H&L projects include being able to tailor the development to your intended end user, their greater depreciation allowances and potential concesssions or rebates.

- The disadvantages of H&L projects include their generally higher cost than other investment types and more competition when selling on.

- Remember – know your endgame before you take on a project to be able to maximise value.

- The physical attributes of the site you want to develop are as just as important as its location.

- Use your dream team to help you understand and compare building contracts and negotiate your buying contract.

- Know your development types: they range from block splits (simplest) to new build strata (most challenging).

- Be prepared for the intricacies of the development cycle: acquisition (including sound analysis of whether a project is worth doing), due diligence, development and construction, and completion (including assessing current market conditions and your investment position to work out whether to action your original goal or change your mind).

## 11

# Commercial property

One of the really amusing things about property investors is that regardless of how savvy they are in the residential space or how complex their dealings have become, many don't feel like serious real estate types until they've acquired at least one commercial holding.

You can almost see them sitting around a bonfire and trading battle stories: 'Sure, mate. You've completed a six-pack apartment project with a retained heritage structure and sublettable common area accommodation... but I own an industrial shed! Commercial investment – now *that's* when you know you're alive!'

Commercial property has its place in a diverse portfolio, but its extreme differences to residential investing mean that it will not suit every investor and their ambitions.

## Why bother with commercial?

Commercial property is really a cash-flow play, because the opportunities to make huge leaps in capital value by buying low and selling high are rare.

Yes, in recent years some commercial investment has done really well for value growth, but if you look across 30 years of data and compare capital gains in commercial and residential, there's no competition – residential will eat commercial alive when measuring value growth.

It's not all that surprising really. Whether it's strata offices, industrial sheds or retail shopfronts, the actual fit-out and floor areas in commercial property tend to be replicated and will not necessarily inspire potential buyers to pay a premium. As hard as you try to boost its cosmetic appeal, a purchaser will not fall in love with a commercial space.

## Commercial vs residential: the differences

Let's take a look at the sort of surprises which will greet any residential investor who flirts with the idea of buying a commercial property.

### Price and rent drivers

As we've already touched upon, the fact that the romance of bricks and mortar may compel some purchasers or tenants to outlay a little extra on a residential property pretty much disappears in the commercial space. That said, if you can understand the drivers that push values and rents in the commercial property sphere, there are ways to differentiate blue-chip investments from secondary options.

The key is understanding what tenants require for their businesses and ensuring your commercial space caters to these.

Let's look at industrial sheds as an example. If the area's industrial tenants are mostly small manufacturers who export parts around the nation or overseas, they are going to require certain essential elements in their building. Access to high-speed internet for running their website and taking online orders will be a priority. They'll also require low-cost, ready access to major transport routes. Road exposure for attracting customers probably isn't an imperative, but a quick trip on a fast highway to other major capitals, or even a no-traffic-lights route to the airport, could be a must.

Speaking of haulage, if there's no room on your site for a transport vehicle to easily manoeuvre into a space where loading and unloading is a breeze, then forget about attracting a premium tenant. Likewise, ceiling height may be a factor for storing materials and supplies, or to allow canopy clearance for larger delivery vehicles.

You get the idea – the factors that propel one commercial site to succeed over another are extremely different to those that drive residential property.

## Finance

Finance around commercial ventures is one of the most surprising aspects for those moving over from residential property.

In commercial lending, the cost of borrowing is higher. You will now be looked after by the commercial division of the financier, where decisions around risk, tenancy security and level of financial exposure mean the lender is factoring in a bit extra in the interest rate, as well as the fees and charges.

Requirements for deposits go up too. There'll be no 95 per cent lend on your new commercial acquisition. Your financier will want to see you tip in some serious dough of your own – often 25 to 30 per cent of the purchase price.

Another factor is how banks treat the loan terms. Most residential investors don't realise that commercial property lenders will require a loan renewal every year or two. That's right – your loan terms are only good for up to a 24-month period. After that, all the documents need to be resubmitted for consideration by your lender. It's again a matter of measuring risk, because the borrower needs to see how the commercial tenancy cash flow is being managed.

## Leases

There are some pros and cons when looking at commercial leases compared to residential leases.

For a start, many residential investors salivate at the idea of commercial tenants paying outgoings and general maintenance. This means that a commercial yield is considered pretty much a net amount rather than a gross amount.

Another great benefit is that commercial leases tend to run over years, with rent rises fixed to particular formulas around measures such as business turnover or CPI.

There are usually options to extend the lease as well. For example, a tenant might be locked in for five years but then have the option to renew for another five. This will seem like a godsend to residential landlords, who never know if they're going to need to look for new tenants every year or so.

However, there is a sting in the tail. Vacancy rates can be extremely high in commercial property. It's not a sector where your tenant leaves and all you have to do is run an open home that'll see three applicants fight for the accommodation. Securing a new tenant can be a long, hard slog. Locking in a five-year lease sounds great, but if I'm getting six months of vacancy after that five-year lease because the tenant decides not to renew their option, can I afford to hold, and is it still a good investment vehicle?

In a downturn, the cheaper secondary stock will cop an absolute shellacking on the letting market, with tenants shopping very hard for the best possible deal. Some landlords even need to offer sweeteners in very soft markets. Offering rent-free periods and extensive fit-outs aren't unusual when trying to woo new tenants.

The reason landlords get desperate is that a vacant commercial property is substantially less valuable than one with a tenant. They're a cash-flow asset, so take away the cash flow and they become much less attractive.

Finding good tenants at reasonable rents and locking them in for the long term is important.

## No romance

Say what you like about buying with the head and not the heart, but most residential property buyers do feel some emotional attachment to their asset. Smart ones don't let it override their common sense, but there's no denying that a walk through one of your properties can give you a glow of pride.

Commercial, on the other hand, is a hard and fast game of numbers. It's all about the buy-in price, rental return and yields. You need to be across lease terms, renewals and inclusions.

It does provide some opportunity for financial minds to flex. For example, you can do some very tasty finance arbitrage if you're savvy. If you can borrow funds at 6 per cent for an asset returning 8 per cent with a 10-year lease attached, that means you are clearing a 2 per cent margin on your outlay. If you've only had to put in a 20 per cent deposit of $100,000 to purchase, that's 2 per cent clear on a $500,000 asset, which isn't too shabby.

## Taxation

Here's where commercial can have it all over residential. The tax rules that apply to commercial investment are very attractive and have been one of the reasons interest in the sector has risen in Australia of late.

Throughout 2017 and 2018, a raft of legislative measures were squarely aimed at curbing property investor enthusiasm. The powers that be determined if investors were to slow down in the residential market, more affordable opportunities would be opened up for first home buyers. Among the changes were moves by APRA to reduce investor lending, introduce legislation that hit foreign investors, and make changes to depreciation rules which reduced the ability for investors to write off expenses in their schedules. Add in state-level tenancy law amendments that increased compliance for landlords, along with increases to land tax and other levees as well. But nobody has been concerned about investment in the commercial space. In fact, commercial property is a golden sector that boosts productivity and economic growth. Just look at the fact that there have never been changes to depreciation rules around commercial property. If part of your plan is to maximise your returns each year, commercial really does start to make sense.

## The dream team

By this stage you'll have grown accustomed to your residential property dream team helping you make big decisions on the right moves in property investment.

However, if you move away from residential and into commercial, you will need a whole new set of advisers with different skills. That extends from the lawyer's perspective – whose understanding of leases and ownership structure will mitigate your risk – through to your finance broker, property manager and investment adviser.

Agents are also very different in the commercial space. Commercial property selling agents tend to take on the mantle of a business broker. While they obviously continue to operate on behalf of the seller, they also know that their buyer will be a seller one day too, so they like to ensure deals are done more equitably than you might perhaps find in residential. They also understand buyers aren't buying a beautiful home with a compelling outlook – they're acquiring a return on investment. Contract negotiations are no longer about comparable sales in the suburb, but become more about what alternative returns you can achieve for your money.

In the end, commercial investment can be an excellent option for experienced investors, but don't just buy into the dream because you're bored of residential property. Buy because it makes sense. Long leases, good tenants and a shortage in a certain asset class are all signs of a reasonable investment option.

Commercial property is a strategic move, not some badge of honour you can flash to non-commercial landlords.

## Chapter Hacks

- Commercial property investing will not suit every investor, as it is extremely different to investing in residential property.
- You'll need to carefully weigh up risks and returns, as both the cost of borrowing and deposit requirements for commercial property are higher, plus loan renewal is required every year or two.
- While commercial leases are generally for at least a few years, note that vacancy rates can be high.
- The tax rules for commercial property are attractive, but seek advice from your dream team (who will need to have specialist commercial property skills and experience) when considering commercial investments.

# PART IV
# MASTERY AND LIVING YOUR BEST LIFE

# 12

# The secret to building long-term wealth

Anything worth having takes effort – frankly, it's no fun if it's too easy. It takes commitment, hard work and tenacity. You need to be able to tackle the challenges, identify the opportunities and change your path as needed.

Learn, grow, adapt... repeat.

We've covered the basics of smart property investing in the previous sections of this book. Getting your head around the different property types, the fundamentals of investing, investor mindset and, most importantly, the need to gain an education while drawing on the experience and expertise of others – this is just the start.

I'd like you to keep all this knowledge front of mind as we look at what I think is one of the key approaches to building a portfolio so your wealth grows at an exponential rate.

Almost anyone can make serious dough out of real estate. If you buy well, don't overextend and wait long enough, the gains in your properties' values will almost certainly exceed your wildest expectations. It's not rocket science – it's just compound growth and common sense.

But I think a golden opportunity is going begging. It's being ignored by the common wisdom and it waits, ready to boost things for you. Best of all, it's a move you can make from day one of your investment journey.

It's the opportunity to buy a property now that holds something in store for your future self. It's the chance to look ahead and realise that you actually can make the most of your money on the way in, because by applying this technique every time you look to add to your portfolio, you can rest easy and keep the long game in mind.

It's called evolutionary investing.

## Evolutionary investing

Like most surfers, I feel some connection with the natural world when I'm sitting among the swell and watching it just be. And I love the way nature allows us to adapt and grow along with our environment. In many ways, through unrushed and measured gain, each step is incremental on its own but substantial as a sum.

The process of slow, steady growth allows us to become mentally and physically comfortable with the state of play before we progress to the next challenge to try, succeed in and learn from. Then, once more, we get comfortable with our 'new normal' before coming across the next challenge to conquer.

This is the foundation of the Darwinian theory of evolution. If you've ever seen that famous graphic which tracks our species' progressive elevation from slack-shouldered apes to majestically upright homo sapiens, you'll know what I'm talking about.

Evolution applies across all aspects of life, including in our investment journey, where we can use it in a successful investing strategy.

## The evolution of the investor

Let's look at the stages of an investor's evolution, with a little surf vernacular thrown in for good measure.

### 1. Grommet

When we begin on our investment path, we are starting with a spark but no flame.

These grommets – or pre-investors – are normally full of enthusiasm for the subject and will devour as much knowledge as possible. They're often obsessed with the possibilities. They haven't yet had to tackle the tough practicalities of things like finance and property selection. Their idealism is enviable.

While I encourage anyone with an interest in real estate, regardless of age, to enter the realm, it would be reasonable to say first-timers are mostly in their twenties, and as an investor cohort they're long-term thinkers who have already mapped out in their mind their plan for leading a life less ordinary.

Pre-investors are generally inexperienced and will require both guidance and understanding. Fortunately, we live in an age when information is just a smartphone away. There are literally thousands of readily available, low- or no-cost sources of knowledge about all sorts of subjects just a few button-clicks away from the average first-timer.

My hot tip for this group is to grasp the chance to learn with all your might, but give nothing away, and do not under any circumstances sign up to a scheme, seminar or property that will cost you a heap of dough. Take the opportunity just to absorb the knowledge.

This is also the time to start building your strategy, as we discussed in Chapters 3 and 4. Make your plans, set your barometer and determine your end point so you can map the steps needed to reach your goal.

## 2. Novice

Members of this group have attained a knowledge level to be able to front up, find a holding, pay the deposit and begin building their portfolio.

First-time investors, for the most part, are at the start of their working life. While they're fairly unencumbered from the responsibilities of having a family and paying a mortgage, first-timers are still great at thinking about the future.

The biggest challenge for first-timers is moving beyond the education and into the reality. Don't become afflicted with paralysis by analysis. Don't educate yourself into a coma!

The reason novices need to take that first step is because time in the market is so important. Opportunities to make great investments come across the desk every day when you're a buyer's agent. Novices can't hold out forever waiting for the perfect property to come along. In fact, the perfect investment is right in front of you, because by actually taking the plunge and acquiring that first holding, you've got your money working for you straight away.

First-time investors need to work with their dream team to be able to manoeuvre into position and get on their board, and then apply what they've learned to take advantage of the waves.

For first-timers, simple initial steps into the property waters are necessary. Novices, just like all investors, need to be across their finance position, and must establish their credentials as reliable borrowers as part of the process.

Property-wise, first-time investors are looking for something straightforward. A well-located unit or house with a solid potential renter base and above-average yield is their best opportunity, with great long-term upside in value an absolute must. Rental returns should be strong to allow some income buffer straight away. In addition, a holding with some opportunity to improve value through renovation or future small development is always handy.

## 3. Talented amateur

For most of us, the first purchase is tough, because there are so many unknowns. But then comes that difficult second investment curse – a time to conquer your fears and overcome psychological obstacles.

As I've mentioned before, the vast majority of investors never own more than one investment. They become overwhelmed, lose focus, lose sight of their goal and throw up their hands in despair, frustration or resignation.

For those who can stick it out, however, this stage is when the foundations of your portfolio really start to solidify. You have put in many of the hard yards and are armed with the sort of practical knowledge about the process that you can only gain via real life experience.

Second- and third-time purchasers also have an opportunity to break free of their comfort zone. You may find that you've gained a bit of equity via your previous investments, so your tolerance for risk, while still realistic, allows you to take a bit more of an educated gamble.

Second- and third-time buyers will perhaps entertain the possibilities of a small renovation project. They'll still stick to areas they feel comfortable with, but might try some more challenging property options with medium-risk, medium-return scenarios.

Their position in the investment world is now established. Talented amateurs occupy a thrilling space in the sector where the possibilities seem endless.

## 4. Expert

Competitive-level investors will have built up some enviable numbers in their investment portfolio. They have the comfort of solid equity and, if they've planned well, will have a manageable cash-flow buffer to play with.

Hopefully, they've earned some bargaining power with the financiers as well. Their track record with the bank is good and their money management skills should be up to speed. They have a decent credit rating and can usually get their broker on the phone to look at a quick deal if the opportunity presents itself.

With a few runs on the board, the expert investor will begin to seek more adventure in their holdings and look to acquire bricks and mortar with a bigger potential twist. These are properties where, with a little imagination, they can make some impressive additional dollars. Expect this more evolved member of the investment species to seek larger blocks with long-term redevelopment potential, or multiple units in small complexes where the gross floor area is being underutilised.

These more experienced investors have a distinct financial advantage over their often younger, less experienced competitors. They have battled for their financial supremacy and now have their choice of the best wave among the pod.

## 5. Pro

The professional-level investor has reached the stage where their portfolio is self-sustaining, and they can make the choice of whether to continue in their paid work life or survive very comfortably off what they've achieved through building their investment cache.

Professional-level investors know their stuff. Their finances are in order, the agents know their name and they are probably pretty good mates with the various members of their dream team.

This group might also be looking beyond residential holdings and starting to dabble in commercial spaces. They'll be learning about all sorts of aspects of real estate at a level well beyond that of their immediate peers.

Given their years spent navigating the rip tides, chops, wedges, tubes and swells of basic property investment, professional-level buyers will be keen to tackle the very top end property types for their portfolio. For example, expect this group to be right into JV projects.

They will also want to build experience in small development projects as they gain proficiency in splitter blocks, speculative home ventures and even unit and townhouse construction projects.

Pros may even choose to experiment with finance structures, using funds from their superannuation or family trust to maximise their outcomes.

Professional investors like to get their hands dirty, take a few risks and blaze a path to success that others can follow.

## 6. Specialist

While professional level is probably the pinnacle clique among investors, I've come across another subgroup which is interesting to observe. Specialist investors have definitely grown beyond the portfolio building stage and have found their niche in one or two aspects of the property sphere.

Specialists like a certain type of investment and will stick with it. They become laser focused on what they want and might even be renowned among their community as the go-to when a particular deal is about to be done.

For example, specialists might like the idea of just tackling high-end renovation projects, or perhaps only attempt new builds on splitter blocks. They might even be specialists in unit or townhouse construction.

The other inspiring element about specialists is that they will also run multiple deals at once. While each deal might be within the same location, price point, property type or development niche, they can all be operating at different levels of completion.

I know of one small developer who has built up a business around doing double block subdivisions in mortgage-belt suburbs with excellent services and facilities. He likes to fly under the radar so let's call him Dave.

Dave creates two titles and then constructs a high-quality home on each block. He's spent years building rapport with agents and contractors so he can bid competitively for sites and negotiate hard on construction costs. Dave will do these deals as a JV and often takes on the project management role while the other JV partner puts up the finances.

On his first deal, Dave achieved a very modest profit margin of just 5 per cent. He reasoned that he was cutting his teeth on the process and wrote off some of the time losses as a learning expense.

That was about 10 years ago. Since then he's honed his skills, struck up competitive contracts with a core set of builders and learned how to streamline his marketing. He now regularly achieves profit margins close to the 20 per cent mark and has between three and five projects running at once. He's also built a reputation as the go-to splitter block guy in his patch.

## It's a marathon

Investors will endure highs and lows throughout their journey – from having a hot water heater blow up or a roof leak, to a full-blown unexpected bathroom renovation in the space of 12 months, to three years of back-to-back double-digit capital growth making them more money sleeping than from their actual job. Long-term investors will experience it all. The best investors help to elevate their community as a whole, providing a beacon of success for others to follow.

If you're just beginning your investment path and are ready to learn, grow, and take the bad with the good, expect to pass through most of these stages of evolution.

## The evolutionary investment

You might have thought all this talk of evolutionary investors was the secret I refer to in the name of this chapter... but it isn't. The secret to creating a highly successful portfolio isn't about your stage as an investor, but rather the ability to pick properties that will be evolutionary investments.

What do I mean by that? Let's take a look.

A mistake many people make is to pigeonhole a property investment as either one thing or another. For example, they are either buying a capital growth detached house in a blue-chip location or a high-yielding unit in a more regional address. They might be purchasing a site that can be split for subdivision or a site that will suit an ancillary dwelling unit. Perhaps they've even evolved to consider a unit development site or their first commercial property.

This constant defining of the lines that contain and restrict each potential investment is, I believe, a huge mistake.

So, from here on out, any time you purchase a property for your portfolio, I want you to ask these two simple questions:

1. What is the potential use for this holding in 10 to 15 years?
2. How does this fit in with my overall plan?

The reason is simply that when you acquire a property – whatever it might currently be – I want you to think about how it will evolve in your portfolio through a property cycle so that in the future you can improve its 'highest and best' use and make even greater gains.

## My first investment

Evolutionary investing is a process you can kick off from day one of your investing journey.

My very first property investment was, somewhat ironically, in Cronulla – the suburb where we now live.

Back in 2008, Kim and I were looking for somewhere to put our feet on the property ladder. We knew it would be in Sydney – I'd done my research and it was certainly the capital city best primed for long-term gains. We were at a stage in the property price cycle where buying was a bit on the nose. Being a counter-cyclical sort of guy, where others whiffed garbage, I could smell opportunity.

And so, the hunt for the right location began. I looked in the southwest market; I looked in the eastern suburbs; I looked at the inner city; I looked at options in the north and northwest out towards Castle Hill and beyond. It was an arduous search, but I was determined. Cronulla had all the locational hallmarks that fit our needs, so then it was on to finding a holding that would cater to our criteria and our budget.

Selecting the asset was always going to come after selecting the location, because if you don't filter your location you will exhaust yourself by travelling far and wide looking at a range of properties in various suburbs but never becoming an expert. Without detailed knowledge of a defined area, it's hard to quickly assess if an investment has potential.

Now that we were locked onto our preferred location, we started unearthing options that would suit our price point and cash-flow parameters. Attached housing certainly looked to be a goer, so we began to hunt for units in earnest.

Now here's the twist, where I was able to apply my approach around evolutionary investing.

How could we purchase a high-yielding, reasonably-priced unit that would evolve over the coming one to three property cycles? The holding needed to be a future asset that had good opportunity for value growth, to outperform its simplistic existing use as 'just a unit'.

The answer was to look for a unit with renovation potential in a complex where the parent lot was large and the older unit complex was an underutilisation of the building's gross floor area. I knew this type of property created options down the track. There would one day be potential for either our body corporate to build additional units or for a developer to come and pay above the odds to acquire the entire complex and redevelop.

This investment has proved a winner already, with the market doing its thing. Compound growth built the asset value to a point where we were able to draw upon a substantial amount of equity gain.

We are also aware, however, that a time will come when we are able to yield even greater return because of our strategic purchase of an evolutionary property.

## Future vision

I've already seen this in action. A valuer associate of mine based in Brisbane purchased a unit in a six-unit, three-storey walk-up complex just outside that city's CBD. It was in an old 1970s block and the unit needed some renovation love, to say the least. What was really interesting to my mate was that while physically inspecting the complex, he noted there were seven obvious units in the complex, despite there only being six units on title. The seventh was designated 'common area' on the registered building unit plan.

Knowing it was a solid investment with good tenant demand, he purchased it in 2005 for $150,000. It turns out 'unit 7' was being rented to a long-term tenant and the rent was being split periodically among the body corporate members – bonus cash flow!

Then in 2010, the body corporate got together and decided to strata off unit 7. With the help of their dream team town planner and solicitor, the collective went through the process. There were some costs, and the local council required a few development conditions to be fulfilled, such as a new wheelie bin area and an upgrade to services, but in the end each unitholder made $50,000 from the deal. And that was after some of the profits were tipped back into the maintenance account for upgrades to the building and grounds, thus improving their overall values even further.

Here's the next bonus – the site's gross floor area is still underutilised. My mate reckons it's only a matter of time before developers start sniffing around this old block with the view to doing a major redevelopment.

Evolutionary investments are everywhere – you just need to know what to look for and be prepared to wait out the cycle once the holding is yours.

Evolutionary investing is yet another example where relying on the experience of your dream team will pay substantial dividends. While I can provide some guidance, you should only proceed under the watchful eye of your expert advisers.

## Six essentials for evolutionary investing

While the concept of evolutionary investing is fairly simple, there are some essential actions you must take to ensure you stay on program and maximise returns.

### 1. Diversify your locations

We all become accustomed to our own patch of Australia. Most people, especially those with a keen interest in real estate, have a profound sense of 'place', an emotional tie to a location that stems from being in familiar territory.

For evolutionary investors, however, it's time to break free of those restrictions and start contemplating bricks and mortar further afield. Across this nation sit 550 local authorities, covering thousands of suburbs and tens of thousands of streets. Evolutionary investors are aware that their best investment options aren't always going to be within walking distance of their front door.

As discussed earlier in this chapter, it's imperative that you decide on location before all else (see Chapter 7 for more about location). Fortunately, we live in an age when it has never been easier to become a borderless investor. The rise of the internet-based real estate market has translated into all sorts of property listings and relevant data being conveniently accessible.

Devote some time to locate your next investment market from across the nation. Read up on the major influencers driving the economy, job growth and increases in population. Consider where the big infrastructure projects are improving living standards. Take a moment to look at where each centre sits in terms of their property price cycle. Choose your locations based on results – not geography.

Once you've successfully determined your region of interest, drill down further. Look at why some suburbs are likely to outperform others. There might be new education facilities being established. There could be a gentrification run just starting, with a few healthy hipster cafés signposting a suburb that's about to become cool. There might be a major piece of transport infrastructure that will bring some suburbs 'closer' to town with reduced commute times.

Once your suburb is locked down, start looking for more nuanced locational elements. You might want to avoid main streets, or locations too close to undesirable uses such as light industrial or service stations. Perhaps you're keen on the property being within walking distance of the local café hub. I've even heard of a street where one side of the road was affected by shifting black soil that played havoc with house foundations whenever it rained, while on the other side of the street… nothing. All was fine!

Start to become the expert on where the better options lie within your suburb of choice.

As is often said, there are markets within markets. Choose your location based on sound analytics and don't be tethered to the idea that you can only buy best in the streets where you live.

## 2. Seek a twist that exists

The next step, once we've hit street level, is to start considering which particular properties hold the most promise.

At this stage you've determined your buy-in budget. The mortgage broker has defined your lending guidelines and you must now seek the best possible options within this price bracket. Start working through the thick weeds of the 'for sale' pages and unearth those investments that will allow you to boost their return via equity gains or rent immediately.

Property that can benefit from cosmetic renovation is a great example of where the end result can see an increase in rental return as well as property value. Another investment might require minor construction work. Perhaps upgrading a downstairs area will yield additional space that can be sublet on a separate title. Units have their own potential too. Removing some internal walls to create open plan living or adding a new benchtop to freshen up the kitchen area can each work in your favour.

Certainly, you should buy well in terms of price, but as an investor I want to ensure there's a chance for me to boost my return from the get-go if possible.

## 3. Seek a twist for the future

Here is when evolutionary investing comes into its own.

When researching a potential investment property, keep an eye out for any indicators that its highest and best use could be even greater in years to come. There is a range of aspects to consider, with variations and combinations that might work together to create an excellent investment option.

Here is a selection of the more common elements that might come into play.

First, **town planning**. Check the zoning or designation of the property. Is the site being fully utilised under current town planning guidelines? We've already discussed examples of unit blocks where the defined allowable gross floor area is not being fully exploited, but there are other options as well.

For example, is the ageing home straddling two separately titled lots? In the current market a split and shift project may perhaps not be profitable, but if not, it's something that could work in your favour in the future.

Perhaps you're looking at a home in an area zoned for unit construction, but your allotment is too small. Could acquiring a neighbouring property at some future date change your detached home into a desirable development site?

While you're working through the town plan, check for local area plans in relation to commercial growth zones, overland flow overlays and demolition control areas. There are all sorts of characteristics in town plans that can help or hinder a property's potential into the next price growth cycle (or two).

The changing **demographics** of a particular location can signpost both price growth and the possibility that housing styles will need to alter to suit a different type of owner or tenant. For example, the establishment of a university or hospital, or expansion of an existing facility, is a great indication of the types of buyers and tenants that will be looking for accommodation locally in the future.

With universities, for instance, comes a rise in demand for accommodation that will allow per-room rental. Look for a home that can be adapted. There might even be changes to the town plan to help increase densities around the facility. Make sure you're hunting for a property that gives you options to capitalise. A large block with space for an ancillary dwelling might be the go.

Keeping an eye on what sort of residents you need to cater for over the coming 10 to 20 years means your holding will always be in demand from both purchasers and renters.

Evolutionary investments will often be defined by their **physical attributes**. The size of a block and its expanse of frontage, along with elevation and topography, are classic measures. Aspect and overall position come into play as well. All of these help to determine what can and can't be created on an allotment.

For example, it's all well and good having an 800 sqm site that falls within a multi-storey high-rise units zoning, but if its dimensions are 10 metre frontage by 80 metre side boundary, there are some obvious impediments to future plans.

In most instances, to give most scope you'll be after a regularly shaped allotment with plenty of useable area. Again, look for where you might be able to take advantage down the track. Perhaps negotiations with a neighbour might see you combine allotments, resulting in a highly desirable option for a developer? Could you negotiate an easement access that would allow you to create a battleaxe, perhaps?

Try to invest in property that has physical flexibilities to be adapted for future use, and look for angles to generate opportunities as well.

## 4. Keep long-term plans in mind

Evolutionary investing requires purchasers to make plans for their future selves. As such, you must always try to factor in to the best of your ability the state of your portfolio and your financial health throughout the investment journey.

This is impossible to tackle with complete accuracy, of course – life will throw up a world of surprises, both great and not so great. There's not much you can do about suddenly losing a job or winning the lotto. At the very least, be aware of where you're heading so you can plan for the long term.

Say a buyer sees an opportunity to purchase a property that's within a precinct earmarked for future development. Terrific! Realistically, a profitable redevelopment of the site might be at least 15 to 20 years off. Demand isn't great at the moment and the location needs a huge boost in employment numbers. Perhaps that's the reason it's so accessibly priced?

Now factor in that this hypothetical buyer is 55 years of age. He is heading toward putting his feet up and spending more time with family. In 15 years' time, at age 70, is he feasibly going to start looking into an arduous development approval process? Not likely.

Conversely, this same investment option might be perfect for a 28-year-old young professional at the start of her career and on the fast track to becoming a partner. You must cater to your age, stage and plans when making evolutionary purchasing decisions.

In your long-term planning, also consider what you might do with your evolutionary investment when the time is ripe. Just because you have neither the means nor expertise to build a six-pack unit project doesn't mean you should avoid the chance to purchase a future development site. There might be options to gain approvals and sell on.

You might even have the chance to take on a JV partner and mitigate risk.

By discussing the possibilities with your advisers and staying on top of the options as they come into play, you will be in the best position to make the right decision when prospects appear.

## 5. Be patient

A key trait among evolutionary investors is the ability to stay the course over the long term. You must position your investments so that you can ride out a property price cycle – or even two – while you wait for all other influences to evolve and help your property reach its peak potential. This means you must factor in ways to keep your investment secure while you're patiently waiting for the right moment.

You will need to land a property with an assured rental income to help service the loan. Don't overextend yourself to the point where a vacancy might tip you into dire financial straits. Make sure there are buffers.

Part of my overall business strategy for my clients is to maximise yield. Buy for gains and boost the rental return. That way, regardless of whether values move up, down or sideways, you can continue to retain ownership without fear of losing the lot.

The real danger comes when investors over-borrow in relation to their income. It's tough to sleep when every spare penny is being sunk into loan repayments just so you can retain your multi-property portfolio. Evolutionary investing is about choosing smarter, not acquiring more.

Patience pays in property. Make sure you can stay in the game.

## 6. Be alert and monitor

While the thought of being lazy and growing wealthy is appealing, the fact is no one made the best possible decisions by taking a set-and-forget approach to property investing.

Smart operators know they must stay on their game to spot the right moments. While time in the market is all-important, don't lose focus: being present and timing your choices can make the difference between a good investment and a spectacular one.

For example, think about the development sites we discussed in point 3. You might be hingeing your decision on the opportunity to purchase your neighbour's house at some future date, thus expanding your holding and increasing its potential. It's a smart move. Statistics suggest that on average, homeowners retain their property for around 10 years. If you are buying with a view to tackling a project in a one- to two-property cycle period, chances are you'll be able to put in an offer at some stage.

However, if you fail to monitor the situation, you might miss your chance. If the neighbour hits the market and signs up a buyer because you haven't kept up regular communication with them or been vigilant for signs of them wanting to sell, then you snooze, you lose. All that initial hard work has been for nothing.

As a smart investor, you will have set up listing alerts on the major portals to know if something of interest becomes available. You should also let the neighbour know at an early stage that you're interested in their property. Make sure you're the first one asked when they feel it's time to sell.

On a personal front, stay ready with your finances. Keep impeccable records and ensure you can act at a moment's notice.

If you are waiting on town planning changes to help create a boosted return on your property, then ensure you monitor the important sources of information. Local authorities will post the progress of planning changes, and your dream team town planner will have other resources to ensure you stay informed.

Be active and make the most of your evolutionary portfolio.

Evolutionary investing is a smart approach to building and maintaining a portfolio that will see you boost your returns. Make sure you apply the property investing principles you have learnt, and lean on your advisers to create a long-term portfolio that will be the envy of other more traditional strategists.

## Chapter Hacks

- Recognise that you're evolving as a property investor: from grommet all the way through to expert and then pro, possibly even to a specialist.

- Evolutionary investing is all about considering a holding's potential use in the long term – through a property cycle or two – and how that fits with your plan.

- You can do evolutionary investing right from the start of your investing journey, as long as you're prepared to wait out the property cycle.

- The six essentials for evolutionary investing are to:
  1. diversify your locations
  2. seek a twist that exists
  3. seek a twist for the future (via elements such as town planning, demographics and physical attributes)
  4. keep long-term plans in mind
  5. be patient
  6. be alert and monitor.

# 13

# Exit strategies

If you've made it this far into my musings, thanks for sticking with me. This chapter is all about the payoff for a journey well-travelled.

For property investors, there are few moments more exciting than when you realise all your hard work and effort has come to fruition. Finally, the financial weight of your investments becomes an opportunity that gives you the chance to live the life you want. At this stage, your portfolio is an open door to fulfilling those planned-for dreams.

Getting out of bed and making the long commute to your nine-to-five job becomes an option, not a requirement. Whether you decide to attend the kids' sports day or take some time off with your significant others is dictated by you and you alone – you are not at the mercy of a boss.

Reaching that point where you are considering your exit strategy is satisfying and liberating. The taste of success is oh so good!

Remember that planning for your exit from property investing is an integral part of the investing journey – but just because it will be the end stage doesn't mean that it is any less important than other stages or should be either ignored or left to chance. Keep your end goal in mind and work towards how best to realise this.

## How much is enough?

Let me be clear: I don't believe there is one correct answer to the question of 'How much is enough?' We humans and our financial affairs are nuanced and complex. We all start at different points and invest with different income levels and household cost requirements. All this financial labour is really about the type of portfolio you build and when you can comfortably move into retirement.

With that said, I'm going to oversimplify some examples purely to illustrate the options.

For discussion purposes in this chapter, I've heard it said that most investors seek a retirement income these days of $125,000 per annum, and many believe a seven-property portfolio will get them there. While I don't completely subscribe to this position, let's use it as a backdrop to our discussion on exit strategies.

Please note: each of the following examples assumes the investor is living in a home that carries no mortgage and has been left out of any portfolio calculations.

## Exit options

When it comes to exit strategies, the options can be a bit daunting. Speak with a handful of different investment advisers and you'll be presented with a variety of plans for reaping your rewards.

I'll discuss a few I've already come across in my time as a property adviser, and then I'll tell you what I consider to be the most satisfying approach to living off your investment portfolio.

### Sell down, pay down

If you read enough articles on real estate investing, you're bound to come across this simplistic approach to exiting, because it seems so mundanely logical.

As an investor, you have been carrying a healthy level of debt. You've structured your portfolio by letting equity build over time and then drawing on that equity to invest again. It's a classic example of time in the market creating wealth.

Let's say, for illustration purposes, that you now own eight properties with a total value of around $6 million. Come age 65, your portfolio has been steadily increasing in value to the point where your loan-to-value ratio (LVR) is about 50 per cent or less. What's next on this program?

This exit strategy simply has you selling down around half of your portfolio to pay out the loans, taxes and other costs on the remainder, and then living off the rental return from your now unencumbered cache of investments.

Here you sit with a net investment portfolio value of around $2.5 million providing a net rental return of approximately 5 per cent per annum, or $125,000. It's not a bad little earner.

As an approach, this has its merits, but there are downsides to consider as well. Let's cover both.

With the sell-down-pay-down exit, you're still holding property that should continue to increase in both value and rental return. This means you can enjoy the benefits of a growing property market for as long as you need.

The portfolio is also debt-free, so you are not at the whim of changes in bank lending policies or the impacts of short-term money markets.

However, this approach requires detailed, long-term planning to ensure you're holding the right mix of income and capital gain assets come retirement time.

In this respect, you are also at the mercy of your various property markets. If you're needing to close out the portfolio debt at a time of depressed prices, this may provide less equity than you'd hoped to clear the loans.

Part of this planning will probably see you flip your investment preferences toward cash-flow property over growth property as you approach the end of your portfolio accumulation phase. Again, you are at the mercy of markets, where timing will play a big role in your eventual success. Pick the wrong cash-flow location at the wrong time and you could do yourself damage.

Another downside to this approach is that selling down a large portion of your portfolio to pay off debt also attracts additional costs by way of tax, commissions and fees. The government will want its share, as will the agents and your advisers. This all eats into a mighty chunk of your net wealth position.

This is why in this option's example, paying down half of your $6 million portfolio leaves you with a net result of $2.5 million.

The sell-down-pay-down approach is a tried and tested method that's seen plenty of success for its devotees, but it's far from perfect, and it can't be applied to the situation of every investor.

## Pure passive income

There are literally volumes written on the subject of creating a portfolio that feeds your passive income. Entire companies of gold-toothed advisers have gotten very rich off helping clients 'grow an amazing portfolio that will have you retiring sooner on $100,000 or more per year'.

This is cash-flow investing at its purest, and the exit is considered a logical outcome to those investors who are devoted to the approach.

As you may recall from Chapter 8, the exponents of cash-flow investing seek properties that will pay them an immediate positive return. The process relies on borrowing for an asset and then using the excess cash flow to help service the loan repayments on your next purchase, which, again, will be cash-flow positive.

By continuing to purchase and refinance, cash-flow investors build enormous multi-property portfolios, with each holding contributing just a little bit of extra income each month to their bank account.

Eventually, the portfolio is generating enough passive income to supplement or exceed your working wage, making it possible to retire.

If you've ever heard of an investor who owns 20 to 30 properties generating a passive net cash flow of $125,000 a year, you've found an advocate of this approach.

Once again, the logic looks sound, but there are pros and cons that must be taken into account.

This seems like a stress-free deal, doesn't it? It suits those who don't have a heap of leftover cash flow in their monthly budget because they are acquiring assets that help pay for themselves and others. It's like some perpetual motion machine of investing that drives on further and further. So, when it works, the strategy removes the worry of having to tip in cash.

The other pro is that you can achieve the passive income position sooner, rather than waiting long term for the market to drive property prices up. So, the exit is simply to reach a point where you stop buying properties and let the excess rent pay for your lifestyle.

The cons of this exit are simply that it can carry extraordinary risks – some of which can ruin you quickly.

As we've discussed, many high-cash-flow properties tend to be in locations with limited capital gains. This means your net wealth via equity come retirement will be comparably miniscule when viewed alongside a capital gain portfolio.

Also, high-cash-flow locations, as a generalisation, can be prone to extreme fluctuations in demand. Take the high cash flows being generated in mining towns a decade ago. If you retired in 2012 on your cash-flow portfolio that was heavy on property in Moranbah, Queensland, you were probably feeling pretty chuffed. However, that same portfolio in 2017 was wrecked – no one was renting, there was no property equity and the bank was knocking on the door.

In addition, the rules around finance can be tough for cash-flow retirees, such as a change to the guidelines and limitation on investor borrowing. For example, if your interest-only borrowing on your highly leveraged cash-flow properties suddenly gets flipped to principal and interest loans on the back of APRA rulings, you might find there's more and more money going out the door each month in loan repayments.

Finally, I believe substantial wealth growth comes from capital gains, not cash flow. For me, being cash-flow positive is just a way to buy time in the market until your capital gains can be fully realised.

Don't get me wrong – a strategy of positive cash flow is an important part of the portfolio building process, but it's not a stand-alone exit strategy that's sustainable in the long term.

## Spend the equity

The world loves an acronym. We've had Yuppies (young urban professionals), Dinks (double income no kids) Sinks (single income no kids) and even Henrys (High earners not rich yet).

One of my other favourites is Skis: spending the kids' inheritance.

This is the realm of those whose exit strategy is to sell down their holdings and live off the equity. Put simply, this exit is used by those investors fortunate enough to have built portfolios full of blue-chip, high-growth assets. They will likely have had to find additional funds each month to cover their loans as they waited through a couple of property cycles, but in the end they've managed to acquire a serious net wealth position.

As an example, say you've managed to lock in a relatively modest $2 million portfolio of high-growth assets. While the rent helps in part to keep the bank at bay, you are having to tip in a little extra.

Regardless of your borrowings, this high-growth portfolio is achieving a compounding value growth rate of 7 per cent per annum and you've been able to hold onto the portfolio through just one property cycle of, say, 12 years.

What would that look like? Well, regardless of rental return and level of borrowings, the value of your portfolio has grown from $2 million to around $4.5 million. Hold out for another cycle and it'll be valued at closer to $10.1 million – this is serious wealth, and you won't get it via cash-flow-only purchases.

The exit is then simply to sell down some assets as needed and live off the profits. When that money runs dry, you can again sell down as needed to pay for your lavish retirement lifestyle.

There are very impressive gains to be made via just buying growth assets. When it comes time to exit, you have a lot of net equity to play with.

If you choose not to sell down all the assets at once, then you also get to continue riding the market's growth until the equity is called upon. So, while you're spending the gains from the first property sold, the rest of the portfolio is continuing to enjoy those above-average-value growth rates that make your balance sheet glow.

The most obvious downside is that you are slowly poisoning the goose that laid your golden egg.

By selling down your holdings and living off the dough, your portfolio is reducing in value, sale by sale. I realise in this instance you have a lot of money to play with, but undisciplined retirees are particularly at risk. If you can't strictly control your spending habits, you're likely to turn around and find your nest egg is gone.

When dealing with a large bank balance, it can be tough to say no to your desires. You might even be tempted into risky business ventures because 'There are all these excess funds at my disposal!' It's a recipe for financial disaster.

This exit also brings with it extraordinary costs in relation to selling out. Like any sell-out strategy, you will be up for CGT and agents' commissions, as well as any bank fees and charges, and other costs along the way. When you're selling out high-value assets, these costs can be amplified, because many are calculated as a percentage of your sell-down figure.

Finally, this approach of eating away at your portfolio relies on you having some idea of your longevity. Sure, no one wants to die with a huge bank balance, but if you create a retirement life that's too lavish, being healthy enough to survive for decades and decades could become a curse to your plans. The money will run out eventually, and while I don't want to appear morbid, you won't want to be around to see your bank balance hit zero.

## Equity drawdown wage

This is a somewhat unusual strategy that will be counterintuitive to those who hate being over-leveraged. I came across it in an article describing how to both retain your high-growth holdings and retire on a handsome post-work income.

The equity drawdown approach is a variation on exiting a high-growth portfolio. Essentially, in this situation you have built a portfolio on the back of choosing high-capital-gain properties and retaining them for as many price cycles as possible.

Come portfolio exit time, rather than selling down any property, the plan is to refinance via a drawdown facility with your preferred lender. You then draw your regular retirement income from this facility. Your loan is secured by the property, and loan repayments come from the drawdown account as well. Your LVR must remain low under this approach to avoid triggering bank concerns.

It sounds diabolically dangerous. You are increasing your debt level through both your cost of living and regular loan repayments. It's like some uncomfortable reversing of the compound capital gains scenario where, instead of value, it's debt that grows exponentially. However, those who subscribe to the process claim its genius lies in the fact that your net wealth continues increasing relative to your debt.

Say your portfolio is worth $5 million debt-free and you set up the loan facility at a 6 per cent interest rate. You draw down $125,000 in year one for living expenses, which costs you $7,500 in interest. Now your net portfolio value would be $4.875 million.

However, your portfolio is structured for growth. Even at a conservative growth rate of 6 per cent per annum, your $5 million portfolio will have gained $300,000 during the year.

The net result? $5 million, less $132,500 in outgoings, plus $300,000 in growth equals $5,167,500.

So, according to this approach you've lived off $125,000 of your equity but even after costs your net wealth has grown by $167,500.

Some think it's a hero idea, but I beg to differ.

The benefits are obviously that you get to continue riding the wave of capital growth by retaining your property portfolio throughout your years of retirement. You enjoy full access to capital gains while still being able to live a $125,000-a-year lifestyle.

The obvious downside to me is that you have a mountain of debt in real dollar terms, and while your LVR might be at a manageable level, having a large number owing against your portfolio can open you up to some serious risks.

First, this sort of increased borrowing and using the loan to service itself is sure to trigger an assessment by the financier at some stage. In retirement under this strategy, you no longer have an independent source of income (such as a job) to show the financier.

Being in a position where your financial survival is absolutely beholden to the bank and its guidelines should make highly leveraged borrowers nervous. And that debt is going to just keep on mounting the longer you live.

Also, low-interest-rate environments obviously work best with this approach. If interest rates shoot up dramatically, as they did in the late 1980s and early 1990s, you will be using more and more of your equity to service the loan. This may again trigger another 'point of intolerability' from the bank.

In addition, a process like this requires extremely great financial discipline. You cannot afford to spend up big – and it will be tempting. The structure literally puts millions of dollars at your disposal. Blow it and your easy retirement life is toast.

I can see the reasoning and understand the mechanics of the approach, but I believe it carries too much risk to be a sensible long-term tactic for retirement.

Looking at the variety of exit strategies should generate healthy discussion around your property portfolio retirement planning. It is in fact an element of the investment process that surprisingly few people consider. Most just blunder through, hoping to make the right decisions when the time comes. However, make the wrong choice and decades of great investing can be put at risk.

## My no-exit exit strategy

I can already hear the cynics saying, 'OK hot shot. You've got a lot of opinions here – what's your bright idea for making the most of your property investments?' Well folks, it's time to come full circle. As I said in Chapter 1, it's all about where you come from. Except this time, I'm talking about when you set your barometer before embarking on the journey.

Property investing shouldn't just be a mindless path to having a bigger bank balance. It should be about making yourself available to participate in the life you desire most.

As you know, for me, property investing buys that precious resource of time with those I love. I don't want to wait until I turn 65 and then find the kids have little interest in spending precious minutes with me. By then, they'll have a range of responsibilities and families of their own. In this scenario, their most enduring memory might be of a father who worked long hours building wealth that he never got to enjoy.

Forget that – I want my rewards now.

I believe with every fibre of my being that if you wait for your portfolio to reach epic proportions before you start yielding your lifelong returns, you're destined to look back with regret. I believe you should start 'retiring' earlier – that is, drawing down your wealth earlier so you can forge your dream life and live it. Don't hold back.

I've been able to achieve my dream life as a result of my evolutionary investment strategy. Through evolutionary investing I have been progressively acquiring strategic assets that have allowed me to ramp up both my equity position and my cash-flow situation. By buying property in the right growth locations with the ability to create additional return – be it via a granny flat, strata project or unit construction – I can choose to retain the assets and boost my cash flow or sell down and reduce my lending.

And I've often bought the asset well in advance and used its rental return to pay down its debt, so by the time it comes to yield its 'X factor' higher use, the profit margins are much greater than if I were buying from scratch. There's no additional stamp duty on purchase and no solicitor's fees or agent involved. I also have the financial wherewithal under this scheme to introduce investments like high-yield commercial into the mix.

So, for me, an exit isn't an exit. It's about managing your portfolio progressively so it graduates from standard residential investment through to projects and a mix of high-yielding assets.

Evolutionary investing is a spectrum that follows through a series of steps – and the paydays come incrementally.

In summary:

1. Make a manageable long-term plan and stick to it.
2. Ensure your cash-flow and equity buffers are firmly in place.
3. Seek cash-flow-neutral or cash-flow-positive investments in growth-zone locations so you can hold long term.
4. Select properties that will evolve into higher uses for future development.
5. Progressively develop and retain or draw down against your investment to support the life you want.
6. Recognise that your barometer isn't really directing you to a gold watch and Maldives holiday.

Holistic investors know that money is freedom to choose. You can't stop the waves, but you can learn to surf.

## Chapter Hacks

- Consider your exit strategy well before time as an integral part of your overall property investing strategy.
- It's up to each investor to work out which sort of exit strategy will best suit their goals and retirement plans – there are pros and cons for each. Your exit strategy should reflect your barometer.
- Exit options include sell-down-pay-down, pure passive income, spending the equity, having an equity drawdown wage and the no-exit exit.
- Try a no-exit exit by progressively developing your portfolio from standard residential through to projects and a mix of high-yielding assets, then drawing down your wealth earlier so you can forge your dream life and live it.

# 14

# Rogue wave – lessons from the pandemic

The following surf scenario has happened to me far too many times.

I have set aside dates in my calendar for one of my regular trips to catch a few waves overseas with friends and family. Obviously, there's the logistics of travel to sort out, but for me there's far more than that to do.

I check my gear and make sure it's all in top-notch condition, replacing and repairing as necessary so nothing fails at a critical moment. I spend weeks preparing physically, whether it be spending time on my home surf break, hitting the gym, going for a run or tackling some specific core work.

I also take time to get my mindset right. I take moments to get excited about the trip – visualising the perfect swell and where to position the board so I can enjoy the ride to its fullest. I'm a big fan of mindfulness, too, so I do regular pre-trip meditation sessions to get present and focused on what I'm about to tackle during the holiday.

The journeys we take to our surf spots are sometimes long and arduous as well – hidden beaches on isolated islands are all part of the adventure.

I'm fully prepared and raring to go. And then, come the big moment... it all falls apart.

A sudden extreme weather event might shut down an airport and make travel impossible. Perhaps conditions will blow out and the swell simply doesn't turn up. There could be an illness or injury which sees my good time get cancelled.

The point is, you can do all the preparation in the world designed to reduce the risks and maximise the benefits, but there will be times when forces beyond your control bring things unstuck.

What I've learned is that in most instances, the solution to these unforeseen challenges is a matter of mindset. For some people an unexpected hitch is a tragedy, but for others it can be an opportunity. A day that can't be spent on the waves could be a prime time to reconnect with old friends over a few beers and leisurely conversation. It can mean additional moments with the kids, teaching them how to surf in the gentler conditions. It could also mean simply a day off to rest, relax, recharge and reformulate your approach for when things come good again.

If you approach these situations the right way, and look to adapt and learn, the eventual outcome may well be even greater success in the future.

And there's never been a better example of this than what has occurred in 2020 and the years since.

## 2020 to 2024 – the years of generational change

For younger readers who are tackling this book for the first time, the global pandemic of 2020 might be a distant memory or just something the 'oldies' still rabbit on about. But the fact remains that COVID-19 was a global event of epic proportions few of us have ever experienced in our lifetimes before – and hopefully none of us will see again.

While the virus is still with us, vaccinations and antivirals have reduced its impact to somewhat the same as influenza – still deadly in some circumstances but manageable for most.

According to www.worldometers.info, daily cases globally peaked at around 3.8 million in January 2022. As at the date of writing there have been more than 774 million cases of the virus and more than 7 million deaths worldwide.

But take a moment to remember a time way back in January 2020 when COVID-19 first reached Australia's shores. We were blissfully unaware of what was to come. Many of us were convinced that this 'bug' would be a temporary event, that somehow we would just 'get over it' in a matter of weeks and things would return to normal.

Then, come March 2020, the rubber hit the road, and everyone was told to stay home. As thing dragged on, there were long weeks, and then months, of lockdowns. There were also lines of unemployed folk seeking benefits, emergency legislation rushed through all levels of government, vaccination programs and toilet-paper hoarding (which seems perhaps the most ridiculous thing of all now). As all these harrowing things dragged on, it became apparent this wouldn't be a short blip on the radar.

Of course, apart from the massive societal toll of this medical emergency, there was also a monstrous economic fallout. Here are few numbers that illustrate the hits:

- Between 21 February and 20 March (that's just 28 days), the ASX 200 plummeted 33 per cent.
- According to the ABS, national unemployment went from 5.1 per cent in February to 7.6 per cent in July. That meant

almost 900,000 Australians found themselves out of a job in a matter of months.

- According to the ABS, $27 billion dollars was wiped off the total value of residential dwelling stock. I can tell you from experience that house prices were quickly discounted anywhere between 5 and 15 per cent during this time. Frankly, those who decided to sell were doing so under the spectre of uncertainty, so they had to take a haircut on their price.

Of course, a raft of legislative assistance kicked in as well. There were extensive subsidies and other measures to help regular citizens maintain a wage, pay their rent and mortgage, and keep food on the table for their families.

One big move to help ease the pain was made by the Reserve Bank of Australia (RBA). As a lever to stimulate the flagging economy and assist businesses and average borrowers, already low interest rates were slashed by the RBA even further. In 2020, the cash rate went from its February level of 0.75 per cent to 0.1 per cent by December, where it would stay right through until to May 2022 – an unprecedented cash rate that many of us are unlikely to see again in our lifetime (which would be a good thing given what prompted the shift).

Of course, emerging from the crisis brought another set of challenges. The bounce back was swift and dramatic. Inflation went from a low of -0.3 per cent in June 2020 to 7.8 per cent by December 2022. Of course, when inflation ramped up quickly and looked like breaching the RBA's target range of between 2 and 3 per cent, the Reserve was prompted to act. After then Governor of the Reserve Bank Philip Lowe said in the first quarter of 2021 that the official cash rate would remain at historic lows until 'at least 2024', the RBA did a backflip come May 2022. A series of increases would see the rate reach 4.35 per cent by November 2023, torpedoing the confidence of everyday borrowers.

## Property market performance under COVID-19

As the first couple of months of the pandemic progressed in 2020, experts were keen to get their property market predictions out to the public.

To say they mostly delivered forecasts full of gloom is a gross understatement. Here's a collation of what high-profile economists foresaw as the likely outcome for real estate markets in response to the pandemic.

In May 2020, both ANZ and Westpac were anticipating Australia's property values would fall by 10 per cent. The NAB were slightly more pessimistic, with a forecast fall of up to 15 per cent. But none could be outdone by Commonwealth Bank, who initially thought a 10 per cent fall would occur, only to triple down in May, going public with a 'worst case scenario' 32 per cent nosedive in house price.

While there were immediate falls in property prices in some markets, the problem with these economic forecasts was their certainty that the value drops would become entrenched. Many commentators at the time were predicting a drawn-out period of depressed values with a recovery unlikely for years and years.

Of course, I concede these people were working in the shadow of the pre-vaccine period, a time when unemployment was skyrocketing while consumer confidence plunged. But let's also remember that major life decisions were being made across the nation on the back of these expert predictions.

Big businesses – including our major financial institutions – pay these specialists huge wages to come up with their outlooks. In addition, average punters across the country were making their own financial plans to cope with what was to come, and most would have been reading these viewpoints in the media with a sense of fear and dread.

So, what actually happened in the months and years following our entry into the pandemic?

A look at CoreLogic's data to 31 May 2021 shows that over a 12-month period, the combined capital-city dwelling value rose 9.4 per cent, while regional values increased 15.2 per cent. That's right – throughout a period when some of the nation's smartest minds determined we should be in freefall, property proved a delightful contradiction!

It wasn't a blip, either. The same analysis in May 2022 revealed an annual price increase of 11.7 per cent for capitals and 22.1 per cent for regionals. It wasn't until May 2023 when dwelling values across both capitals and regionals fell by around 7.0 per cent on the annual measure, but given the extraordinary gains since the start of the crisis this still shows a net result over the three years of about 14 per cent increase for capital cities and a staggering 30 per cent for regionals.

So, why didn't the predicted price falls come to pass? Well, several factors combined to create a situation where high demand met low supply.

For starters, myriad factors drove demand. Government policy kicked into gear with incentives and handouts. In addition to direct financial assistance for households, schemes such as the Homebuilder grant (which was designed to stimulate construction activity) gave people more confidence to get active buying, building and renovating.

In addition, major financial institutions came to the party, allowing households to defer their repayments, which helped bolster family cash flows. This, combined with the RBA taking interest rates to the chopping block during the pandemic itself, also allowed Aussies to feel less stressed about income security.

The other fact is that while shutdowns were underway, no one was spending their money on disposable income items. War chests of savings were being built in households across the nation – money put aside 'just in case things get worse'. ABS data shows between December 2019 and June 2020, total household deposits (money set aside) tripled.

So, here we have cashed-up property buyers being incentivised to act in order to stimulate the economy and secure a roof over their heads.

The other huge factor which has played into property market performance more recently has to be the immigration story, especially its impact on the rental market.

The boom gates were brought down on our international borders in 2020. Our net long-term average immigration number went from approximately 225,000 to effectively zero overnight – and it was kept that way pretty much until November 2021, when we started a slow reopening of the nation. Come February 2022, we were back to allowing vaccinated arrivals entry to Australia.

With businesses screaming out for workers, once the gates were reopened we saw a staggering rush to our country. Over half a million new arrivals came to our nation by June 2023, and many predict it will be similar number in 2024 too.

All these folks need housing – mostly in rentals, but also as owners. They've arrived during a time of extreme rental demand and a building shortage brought on by rising construction costs.

On the other side of the ledger is supply – and the uncertainties of the crisis led to one intrinsic truth, which is that's those who enjoyed the security of home ownership didn't want to rock their boat. Put another way, property owners who didn't need to sell simply decided not to – even if they'd had plans pre-pandemic to do so.

CoreLogic analysis shows that in 2020, new listings numbers halved between March and May. While listings did gently rise over subsequent months, they remained stubbornly below the 50,000 to 55,000 new listings seen in the first quarters of 2015, 2016, 2017 and 2018.

It looked like listings would start to trend back to normal as we passed through November 2021, but interest rate increases the following year delivered another shock – and sellers went to ground once more. By October 2022, new listings were back down below 35,000, and they've pretty much stayed below long-term average right through until early 2024 (when interest rate rises peaked).

New housing supply has also been stymied in the past four years by an extreme construction shortage brought on by elevated building costs. The global shutdown of production, and related limits to shipping, meant the supply chain of materials became slower and more expensive throughout the pandemic. In more recent times, materials have become less expensive, but demand for qualified tradespeople has ramped up. In short, it's been difficult to build new housing affordably, and this has led to lower supply, feeding a very hungry market.

## Lessons from the crisis

As I said back in Chapter 5, diamonds are made under pressure.

For those who've lived through this extremely testing pandemic period and its tough recovery, there have been some extraordinary lessons, both personal and about the world more broadly. I think there are some fabulous learnings we property investors should take heed of – and they all speak to the wisdom of choosing real estate as the prime vehicle for achieving financial freedom.

Here are my six big takeaways for investors from these tumultuous four years.

## 1. Fundamentals reign supreme

Speculation by economists and other observers about the impending doom of a property market collapse proved entirely wrong for one simple reason: supply versus demand.

Political and societal response to the pandemic created a situation Australia-wide where there simply wasn't enough shelter for our population. This was magnified as we reopened ourselves to the world and took in more folks from across the oceans while having too few places to accommodate them.

So long as demand exceeds supply in any property market, prices (and rents) will rise.

While it has already been well demonstrated on a national level since 2020, you can take this thinking to the bank on more nuanced locational analysis too. Through detailed research, it is possible to pick those locales earmarked for a favourable demand–supply imbalance: those set to attract more population. Perhaps an increase in residents will be driven by a new or growing industry base offering employment. Maybe it will be gentrification of an area or the establishment of great local facilities. Big infrastructure projects – especially in the transport space – will make some areas more accessible by reducing commute times to major employment hubs. Buy before the project is completed and you will reap the rewards.

All in all, if you pinpoint a location where supply will sustainably exceed demand, you are on your way to a winning investment.

## 2. Illiquidity is a blessing, not a curse

There are situations where it's important to have liquid assets and ready cash on hand. Emergencies arise and access to funds is key. But for those assets where a long-term mindset is essential to success, illiquidity can keep your strategy in check.

In the initial months of the COVID-19 crisis, there would have been enormous pressure on property investors to sell down their assets and shore up their cash positions. Those owners who were stymied by the slow real estate selling process should be thanking their lucky stars that property is an illiquid asset.

Why? Well, look at the stock market. A 33 per cent fall in 28 days shows just how frightened investors became, and because shareholders could sell off quickly, the pain of loss was immediately realised. This is just the sort of reactionary asset class that can fluctuate in value from calm to cyclonic in a matter of hours.

In contrast, property investors must move at a more glacial pace. Marketing a home properly is a multi-week process. While some owners may have needed to sell at a bargain price, most were forced to 'take a moment' and catch their breath so they could make more reasoned decisions.

This illiquidity means property is less subject to extreme fluctuations in value. It is an even-tempered gauge of economic performance in that respect. It offers surety, security and resilience, which is ideal for long-term investing strategies.

Of course, most expert investment strategies require the investor to keep a war chest of available funds on hand to deal with the unexpected. This stash of ready cash might be held in a home's offset account, for example, so that when it's needed all the bills can be covered at short notice without fear of draining your asset base.

## 3. Experts can be wrong too

Many years ago, I had a colleague who used to say, 'Economists? Well… they get things right about half the time!'

Never has this been better illustrated than with predictions made about how property prices would fare during the pandemic.

I still wonder how the Commonwealth Bank advisor who predicted a worst-case scenario of values falling 32 per cent is doing at work.

While some might think these expert commentators should be skewered for being so far out of kilter with their COVID-19 property market predictions, the truth is that all any of us can do is work with the information we have on hand at the time we are making our decisions. I actually think it's a bit rich for people in hindsight to attack those who had to make a call on something in the midst of a seismic event.

What I will say is that when it comes to property, don't believe everything you read. Much of what makes news headlines is designed to grab eyeballs, not present well-reasoned advice. There are ways to mitigate risk, even when the world seems to be falling apart. The most successful way to keep safe is to invest in the right kind of assets for your circumstances and with a long-term vision.

Of course, you should rely on specialists in the property acquisition space to identify those holdings that have the right fundamentals. Well trained, independent advisors can help keep your wealth base safe through strategic purchasing.

## 4. Australian housing is a protected species

Some of you might remember the global financial crisis (GFC) of 2007 and 2008, when there was a real risk the entire US financial system would implode, with some centuries-old banking institutions on the brink of collapse.

The then federal government in the USA stepped in with assistance to ensure that wouldn't happen. Why? Because the banking industry is 'too big to fail'. Banks are so large, and the financial sector so interconnected, that their downfall could very well have brought the entire US economy to a disastrous end.

While Australian property is not of the same order of magnitude as the American banking system, in terms of our nation's wealth, real estate is the clear leader.

According to CoreLogic, in February 2024 the total value of Australian residential real estate was $10.3 trillion. In comparison, Australian superannuation was worth $3.5 trillion, Australian listed stocks were worth $3.0 trillion and commercial real estate was valued at $1.3 trillion. So, residential property is almost three times more valuable than any other asset class in the country.

In addition, the real estate sector employs millions of Aussies either directly or indirectly. From property managers and builders through to cleaners and tradespeople, our country's residential real estate fills the pay packets of an enormous number of citizens.

Its sacred status was well and truly confirmed by the pandemic crisis. As soon as danger loomed, governments across all tiers sought to quickly implement policies to ensure as few people as possible would be forced into offloading their property assets at discounted prices. Major financiers and the RBA all came on board too. The result was that most owners rode out the storm with their property portfolios intact. In return for that assistance, the industry has remained one of the biggest employers and contributors to taxation in the nation.

An investment in Australian residential property does come with risk, but there is always a political appetite to ensure it remains robust as an asset class, because the consequences of its failure are unfathomably dire for the entire economy.

## 5. Long-term strategies work

One of the most important lessons from 2020 to 2024 is that tenacity pays when you're a property investor. Sticking with the long-term plan, not being distracted by short-term blips, is what divides success from failure.

As I mentioned earlier, the inherent illiquidity of property helped save thousands of homeowners from making a rash decision to sell when things looked dire. That said, there was a raft of people who still looked to sell down assets they could have retained.

The numbers detailed earlier in this chapter tell the story. The national median capital city home value at the height of the pandemic in July 2020 was $637,270. Come February 2024 (post-pandemic) it was $842,109.

Anybody who panicked and sold down during the pandemic in these markets would have missed out on approximately 32 per cent in capital growth over the past four years – but that's just on average across all capital cities. If you'd sold in Perth you'd have missed 56 per cent value growth, Brisbane would have been a 60 per cent opportunity loss, and in Adelaide the missed gains would have been 65 per cent.

By not staying the course and adopting a long-term mindset, those sellers have been out of the market during a period of incredible growth – and all during a global pandemic that was supposed to mean the end of economic stability.

## 6. There's more than one market

Smart property market analysis is about more than just seeing dire economic news and deciding that all Australian real estate prices will collapse.

As has been demonstrated time and again, different locations, property types and price points perform differently. I demonstrated that complexity in Chapter 7, but the pandemic period has further illustrated the effect.

For starters, regional markets shone during COVID-19. As the population decentralised away from higher-density capital cities, those regional centres – particularly those with lifestyle benefits, like coastal locations – absolutely flourished. Regional populations swelled, industry went remote, workers were productive from home and real estate in these once-isolated locations skyrocketed in value. Statistically, for the first time in living memory, almost all regional areas consistently outperformed capitals in terms of price growth.

Then there's the impact of immigration and the rental crisis. Lower-priced properties – including second-hand units – are incredibly popular as migrants come back into Australia. These affordable property types in close proximity to CBDs are easy to get tenanted. Their low buy-in price is also attractive to a large number of purchasers, including first homebuyers, investors and anyone looking to escape the rental market. Prestige property is doing well too, with cashed-up expats and those who made serious money during the pandemic now eager to spend on ultra-luxe homes.

Then there's the downturn in the once-popular renovator market. High construction costs mean there is little appetite for these types of properties at present (but their time will come).

The point is that Australian real estate is a complex tapestry of different markets. With the right guidance, you can identify the locations, property types and price points that are likely to perform best under whatever prevailing conditions there are. You just need to look past the 'one size fits all' predictions and rely on nuanced advice from a specialist analyst.

*

The upshot is this: any time is the right time to invest in Australian real estate if you have the right mindset and guidance. Our own office conducted analysis which looked not just at the current crisis but also Australia's past five recessions going back to the 1980s. Our numbers showed that average price growth after each of the past five recessions was approximately 33 per cent – and all indicators at that time pointed towards a property growth cycle as opposed to a huge decline in property values.

In short, what has happened in the past is likely to happen again, and that is due to the natural market forces that occur during recessions, such as cheaper money, fiscal stimulus across many different verticals and, ultimately, artificially induced economic growth.

In my experience, the biggest financial losses aren't caused by choosing to invest but are rather the result of inaction and fear.

# Postscript:
# The life you want

There are so many rivers to cross in life's travels. While it may sound clichéd, I firmly believe the reward is defined by the journey, not the destination.

Too many people lose sight of what's around them along the way. Their focus on the outcome means they ignore those diamond moments that every one of us can experience if we only pause and appreciate life as it's happening.

Of all the information and advice in this book, perhaps the most important I can pass on is to make sure you are a holistic human being. Investment for financial security is an important part of the mix, but money is not the destination, it's the vehicle for creating the life you want.

## Life's three pillars

If you want to feel fulfilled by good fortune, there are three pillars of life that require ongoing attention.

### Health

You do not want to be the richest person in the graveyard.

There is no sugar-coating the fact. The world is littered with unhealthy rich capitalists whose unabashed obsession with wealth has left them ignoring the most basic need for a happy life: good health.

I challenge you to name one multi-millionaire who, near the end of their time and wracked with illness, wouldn't give their entire fortune to have their health back. You cannot enjoy the fruits of your labour if all the effort and exertion has left you unable and unwilling to take care of the body you've been blessed with.

## Wealth

You wouldn't be wandering through these pages if you weren't motivated by building personal wealth to create the life you want.

Along with your own physical wellbeing and personal relationships, pay attention to your pecuniary wherewithal. Lean on those around you – both friends and paid advisers – so you can get the best out of your financial situation.

## Happiness

Not making time to be happy is often the single biggest mistake made by anyone whose life has become a mediocre personal feedback loop of daily waking, working, eating, sleeping… repeat ad infinitum.

As pleasant as a cycle of familiarity can be, it starts to wear thin. Find ways to surf beyond the mundane. Otherwise, you'll eventually work yourself into an unhappy circle if you don't break out of it every now and then.

What's most important is to plan it – don't be reactive. Don't be a person who thinks, 'Shit! I'm unhappy. I've got to do something…' Don't get to that stage. Take out your calendar, rally your troops and say, 'Let's do this!' It gives you something additional to live for.

The Scottish writer Alexander Chalmers is attributed with saying, 'The three grand essentials of happiness are: something to do, someone to love, and something to hope for'.

Happiness is a noble pursuit. It's certainly not trivial, so don't neglect this important pillar of life.

## Six practical moves for creating the life you want

I have some essential habits that help me maintain the three pillars of life. They are practical exercises anyone can adapt and apply to maximise their existence and gain peak enjoyment from all the opportunities they've created via their investment decisions.

### 1. Health focus

I make sure health is as much of a priority in my day as my work and my relationships.

Set aside an hour a day, five days a week, to concentrate on doing something that boosts your wellness. Run, swim, walk, surf, do yoga, go to the gym… whatever works best for you.

I don't see this time as a task – it's actually become a ritual opportunity to take a break from work and indulge in something that makes me feel alive. And for anyone who says they don't have time in their schedule for exercise, just make it. I guarantee you will be more productive and connected at work, and more relaxed and engaged at home, as a result.

Daily exercise will boost your output, not hinder it.

### 2. Happiness break

One absolutely locked-and-loaded essential in the process that boosts both mental and physical wellbeing for me is a surf trip with my mates every six months – without fail.

As I write this, I'm making plans for the next journey overseas. My circle of friends take these expeditions with me every half year to recharge and appreciate how fortunate we are in our lives.

They're planned well ahead and set in the calendar. They help remind me what's important and what we do all this hard work for. While I am all about family first, these trips provide something different to look forward to.

## 3. Personal development time

I put aside two days every six months to devote to my own personal and professional development.

They are guaranteed dates when I will physically remove myself from my regular place of business and my home. Each development day is dedicated to learning something new that will help me become an even better human being.

In the past, I've used this time to become an accredited trainer in Stephen Covey's *7 Habits of Highly Effective People* and in the Herrmann Brain Dominance Instrument®, which is a measure to describe people's thinking preferences.

I have a mate who works in communications and made time for a writer's retreat so he could work on his sitcom script. Laugh at the material but not him – it was a very smart thing to do.

Whatever you choose to concentrate on, there needs to be no distractions. Get out of what you're normally doing and commit to it. And it doesn't have to be overseas or interstate – it can be within 10 minutes of your front door.

## 4. Select the company you keep

Carefully choose the people you surround yourself with, because you will become the product of the five people closest to you.

That doesn't mean if you hang around five professional rugby players, you will be able to sign a first-grade contract with the NRL. It just means you should align the different aspects of your life to a group that encapsulates the traits you wish to emulate.

Have a great group of property mates who've done the hard yards in the investment space. Similarly, with your exercise, train with a group of people whose dedication to hard effort and results has gained your respect. I like to surf with the same gang on each trip so we challenge each other and enjoy our time together.

Pick these groups for each of the important buckets in your life and stick by them so you learn and grow in their wake.

### 5. Keep good habits

When I worked in London I remember a dean of a high school quoting Aristotle, saying, 'We are what we repeatedly do. Excellence is not an act, but a habit'.

It was at a stage when I was about to return to Australia. It really hit home that I didn't apply this theory enough, so I took up the challenge and brought it back with me as a personal mantra.

I want my habits to be good habits – and you should too.

### 6. Be an absorber

Accept that in all aspects of your day, there will be people who have something to teach you.

I'm not out here proclaiming to be the messiah of property, for example, because ultimately, I don't know everything and I never will. That's why I love hearing other people's opinions. Often they're coming to me with a different level of understanding or a certain take on things that I've never considered.

Be a sponge and soak it all in.

### And so it goes...

There are times in your life when everything comes together – the hard work, focused approach and careful planning all align.

Sitting among my favourite breaks, there's a chance to reflect on it all. How did we get to this very moment? The odds were surely stacked against us. The sheer fact that we exist is equivalent to gambling probabilities that seem unfathomably long-shot: surviving, learning and growing from the years of parental dependence through to when we introduce our own offspring to the world, a new generation to be armed with knowledge for life's challenges.

Floating in the swell, I even like to ruminate on the smallest facets. Being able to climb on my board and paddle out, pitch the nose and enjoy the ride with little fear and maximum delight is the culmination of many days of trial, failure and learning... to succeed. Reset your high bar and go again. Anything worthwhile takes effort.

And while I said in Chapter 1 that there's no escaping where you came from, where you eventually end up is almost entirely up to you.

As property investors, we take on all sorts of challenges and risks. While I'm a huge fan of having limited stress, there's no avoiding the fact that taking the steps to reach your goals requires leaps of faith from many take-off points along the path.

Yes, it's good to remember where you came from, how you got here and where you are going.

# Glossary of terms

**APRA.** Australian Prudential Regulation Authority, the regulator of the Australian financial services sector.

**BA.** Building application, also known as *building permit*. The BA consists of paperwork you submit to secure a building approval.

**Block split.** A site held under a single title but which is already described by two or more lot numbers. Under this arrangement, an investor may choose to go through a process of retitling that will result in separate titles being issued for each lot or block.

**Capital gains tax (CGT).** The tax you pay on the profit from an investment after you have sold it. Note: CGT does not apply to profit on the sales of you own home (principal place of residence).

**Compound growth.** Growth you can achieve if you reinvest the income and profits you receive from your initial investment. Compound growth can fast-track the return on your investment.

**CPI.** Consumer price index, also know as the rate of inflation.

**DA.** Development application or development approval. A DA is lodged with council to ensure your proposed building work meets all necessary planning requirements.

**Dual-income-style properties.** These are properties with a granny flat, so the owner receives rental income from the main dwelling and the second smaller residence.

**Equity.** When talking about property, equity is the value of your ownership. For example, if you own a property valued at $500,000 and have a mortgage of $200,000, then you have $300,000 or 60 per cent equity in that property.

**Equities.** Also known as shares or stocks, equities are shares in a company, usually those listed on the stock exchange.

**Grommet.** Surfing slang meaning a young surfer.

**H&L.** House and land project. In this book H&L refers to an endeavour to construct an entirely new home on a standard-size vacant residential allotment.

**Holding costs.** The cost to hold vacant land or a property under development, which is not generating any rental income.

**JV.** Joint ventures.

**Leverage.** Another word for *borrowing*. When used in relation to property it means using borrowed funds to increase the returns from your investment.

**LVR.** Loan-to-value ratio.

**Overcapitalisation.** When you spend more on renovating or developing a property than the increase will be in the value of the property after the renovations.

**Rentvesting.** A term used to describe the strategy of buying an investment property while continuing to rent in another location.

**STCA.** Subject to council approval. STCA is used when marketing a property that has the potential to be developed but no planning applications have yet been lodged to test this assumption.

**Strata title.** A form of property ownership devised for multi-level apartment blocks and subdivisions with shared areas.

# Index

**Be better with business books**

**MAJOR STREET**